p 22

LEADERSHIP
AND
MOTIVATION

LEADERSHIP AND MOTIVATION

The fifty-fifty rule and the eight key principles of motivating others

JOHN ADAIR

KOGAN PAGE

London and Philadelphia

Publisher's note

Every possible effort has been made to ensure that the information contained in this book is accurate at the time of going to press, and the publishers and author cannot accept responsibility for any errors or omissions, however caused. No responsibility for loss or damage occasioned to any person acting, or refraining from action, as a result of the material in this publication can be accepted by the editor, the publisher or the author.

First published in Great Britain in 1990 by the Talbot Adair Press as *Understanding Motivation*
This edition published in Great Britain and the United States by Kogan Page Limited in 2006 as *Leadership and Motivation*
Reprinted 2007

120 Pentonville Road
London N1 9JN
United Kingdom
www.kogan-page.co.uk

525 South 4th Street, #241
Philadelphia PA 19147
USA

ISBN-10   0 7494 4798 2
ISBN-13   978 0 7494 4798 4

British Library Cataloguing-in-Publication Data

A CIP record for this book is available from the British Library.

Library of Congress Cataloging-in-Publication Data

Adair, John, 1934–
    Leadership & motivation : the fifty-fifty rule & and eight key principles of motivating others / John Adair.
        p. cm.
    Includes bibliographical references and index.
    ISBN 0-7494-4798-2
    1. Leadership. 2. Motivation (Psychology) 3. Employee motivation. I. Title.
II. Title: Leadership and motivation.
HD57.7.A2754 2006
658.4'092—dc22

2006016469

Typeset by Jean Cussons Typesetting, Diss, Norfolk
Printed and bound in Great Britain by Creative Print and Design (Wales), Ebbw Vale

Contents

The two great movers of the human mind are the desire of good and the fear of evil.

Samuel Johnson

About the Author

John Adair is now widely regarded as the world's leading authority on leadership and leadership development. The author of 30 books on the subject, he has been named as one of the 40 people worldwide who have contributed most to the development of management thought and practice.

Educated at St Paul's School, John Adair has enjoyed a varied and colourful career. He served as adjutant in a Bedouin regiment in the Arab Legion, worked as a deckhand on an Arctic trawler and had a spell as an orderly in a hospital operating theatre. After Cambridge he became Senior Lecturer in Military History and Leadership Training Adviser at the Royal Military Academy, Sandhurst, before becoming the first Director of Studies at St George's House in Windsor Castle and then Associate Director of the Industrial Society. Later he became the world's first Professor in Leadership Studies at the University of Surrey. He also helped to found Europe's first Centre for Leadership Studies at the University of Exeter.

John Adair now acts as a national and international adviser on leadership development. His recent books, published by Kogan Page, include *Not Bosses But Leaders*, *The Inspirational Leader* and *How to Grow Leaders*.

Introduction

What motivates people – what makes them tick – is a subject of perennial fascination. It is especially important for practical leaders in industry, commerce and the public services – and indeed to anyone who works with other people – to think about this question in some depth.

What is motivation? A man or woman is motivated when he or she WANTS to do something. A motive is not quite the same as an incentive. Whereas a person may be inspired or made enthusiastic by an incentive, his or her main motive for wanting to do something may be fear of punishment. Motivation covers ALL the reasons which underlie the way in which a person acts.

Two US professors of psychology – Abraham Maslow and Frederick Herzberg – have made major contributions to our understanding of motivation. Our common phrase 'job satisfaction' arose largely from the work of the latter. Maslow is now the world's most influential psychologist after Freud and Jung. The time is ripe for a review of their contributions to motivational theory in the light of the needs of today.

In my judgement no other comparable studies of motivation to those of Maslow and Herzberg have emerged from other authors. Or, rather, they have emerged but not stayed the course. Maslow and Herzberg have stood the test of time. This fact does not, of course, guarantee them, but it does at least suggest that there is a large element of truth in them. For, as Albert Einstein once said, 'Truth is that which stands the test of experience.'

This book goes beyond Maslow and Herzberg, however, and it offers a new general theory of motivation. My reflections on Maslow and Herzberg over the years, in the context of developing the Action-Centred Leadership (ACL) model, have led me to formulate the Fifty-Fifty Rule. Put simply, it proposes that 50 per cent of our motivation is inner-generated, while 50 per cent comes from outside of us.

The real point of the book, of course, is to stimulate your own thinking and ideas on this most interesting of all subjects. It should lead you to see some practical ways in which you can better motivate yourself and others.

You will notice as you read that the texture of the writing varies. I should explain that my discussion of the contributions of Maslow and Herzberg is based on part of a thesis that I submitted at Oxford University for a higher research degree. Work of this rigorous kind is very important in leadership studies and I make no apology for it. But in this context you should feel free to skip any pages that seem to be telling you more than you need to know.

This book is not designed for an academic purpose. It is written for thoughtful leaders, those who wish to work with the grain of human nature rather than against it. I know that I shall enjoy sharing with you what I have discovered about leadership and management – I hope that you will also enjoy our journey together in these pages.

PART 1

Leadership and Motivation

1

Functional Leadership

Leadership is action, not position.

Donald H McGannon

Leadership and motivation are like brother and sister. It is difficult to think of a leader who does not motivate others. But leadership embraces more than motivation.

What is leadership? The Action-Centred Leadership (ACL) approach offers a comprehensive answer to that question. The model encompasses the concept of Individual Needs, which is the area chartered by Maslow and Herzberg. Therefore it provides a natural context for an exploration of their theories in Part Two. In this chapter I shall outline the original content of ACL.

THE BACKGROUND

Functional Leadership training was first developed at the Royal Military Academy, Sandhurst as part of a programme introducing young officers to the responsibilities of leadership. When transposed into industry and commerce it was renamed Action-Centred Leadership (ACL). Initially, the core content of ACL remained much the same as the original Sandhurst version, though the practical exercises and case studies where changed.

In this introductory chapter I shall present the framework of that original concept of ACL, and then comment upon its constituent elements in the following chapter.

My standard introduction to the ACL model has been to look first at the Qualities Approach and then at the Situational Approach to leadership. Having outlined these approaches or theories, identifying both their drawbacks and their positive contributions to our understanding of leadership, I move on to the third ingredient in the story (apart from the personality and character of the *leader* and the *situation* in which it was all happening), namely the *people* concerned. Having mentioned the amount of research done on groups as wholes that are more than the sum of their parts (which led to the establishment of the new sub-discipline of Social Psychology) I explain that I have selected one theory from the mass of research material which I consider to be of most relevance to the practical manager intent upon understanding leadership and motivation – the theory of *group needs*. To this I add the concept of *group personality*. This is how I actually explain it.

THE THEORY OF GROUP PERSONALITY AND GROUP NEEDS

As a starting point I have developed the idea that working

groups resemble individuals in that although they are always unique (each develops its own 'group personality') yet they share, as do individuals, certain common 'needs'. There are three areas of need present in such groups. Two of these are the properties of the group as a whole, namely *the need to accomplish the common tasks* and *the need to be maintained as a cohesive social unity* (which I have called the 'team maintenance need'). The third area is constituted by the sum of the *individual needs* of group members.

INDIVIDUAL NEEDS AND MOTIVATION

This third area of need present in the corporate life inheres in the individual members rather than in the group itself. To the latter they bring a variety of needs – physical, social, intellectual and spiritual – which may or may not be met by participating in the activity of the group. Probably physical needs first drew men together in working groups: the primitive hunter could take away from the slain elephant a hunk of meat and a piece of hide for his own family. Nowadays the means for satisfying these basic needs of food, shelter and protection are received in money rather than in kind, but the principle remains the same.

There are, however, other needs less tangible or conscious even to their possessors which the social interaction of working together in groups may or may not fulfil. These tend to merge into one another, and they cannot be isolated with any precision, but Figure 1.1 will indicate their character. Drawn from the work of A H Maslow[1] it also makes the point that needs are organized on a priority basis. As basic needs become relatively satisfied the higher needs come to the fore and become motivating influences.

Physiological	Safety	Social	Esteem	Self-actualization
				Growth
			Self-respect	Personal development
	Safety	Belonging	Status	Accomplishment
Physiological	Security	Social activities	Recognition	
Hunger	Protection from danger	Love		
Thirst				
Sleep				

Figure 1.1   *The priority of needs*

These need spring from the depths of our common life as human beings. They may attract us to, or repel us from, any given group. Underlying them all is the fact that people need one another, not just to survive but to achieve and develop personality. This growth occurs in a whole range of social activity – friendship, marriage, neighbourhood – but inevitably work groups are extremely important because so many people spend so much of their waking time in them.

Professor Frederick Herzberg has dichotomized the list by suggesting that the factors which make people experience satisfaction in their work situation are not the reverse of those which make them dissatisfied. The latter is caused by deficiencies in the environment or context of the job; in contrast, job satisfaction rests upon the content of the work and the opportunities it presents for achievement, recognition, professional development, and personal growth.[2]

THE NEEDS INTERACT

The first major point is that these three areas of need influence one another for better or worse. For example, if a group fails in its task this will intensify the disintegrative tendencies present in the group and produce a diminished satisfaction for its individual members. If there is a lack of unity or harmonious relationships in the group this will affect performance on the job and also individual needs (cf. A H Maslow's Social Needs). And obviously an individual who feels frustrated and unhappy in a particular work environment will not make his or her maximum contribution to either the common task or to the life of the group.

Conversely, achievement in terms of a common aim tends to build a sense of group identity – the 'we-feeling', as some have called it. The moment of victory closes the psychological gaps between people: morale rises naturally. Good internal communications and a developed team spirit based upon past successes make a group much more likely to do well in its task area, and incidentally provide a more satisfactory climate for the individual. Lastly, an individual whose needs are recognized and who feels that he or she can make a characteristic and worthwhile contribution both to the task and the group will tend to produce good fruits in both these areas.

We can illustrate these interrelations with a simple model:

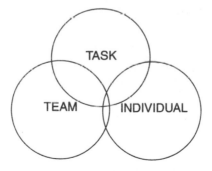

Figure 1.2 *Interaction of needs*

If you place a coin over the 'Task' circle it will immediately cover segments of the other two circles as well. In other words, lack of task or failure to achieve it will affect both team maintenance, eg increasing disruptive tendencies, and also the area of individual needs, lowering member satisfaction within the group. Move the coin on to the 'Team' circle, and again the impact of a near-complete lack of relationships in the group on both task and individual needs may be seen at a glance.

Conversely, when a group achieves its task the degree of group cohesiveness and enjoyment or membership should go up. Morale, both corporate and individual, will be higher. And if the members of a group happen to get on extremely well together and find that they can work closely as a team, this will increase their work performance and also meet some important needs which individuals bring with them into the common life.

These three interlocking circles therefore illustrate the general point that each area of need exerts an influence upon the other two: they do not form watertight compartments.

LEADERSHIP FUNCTIONS

In order for the needs in these areas to be met in any group or organization certain *functions* have to be performed. According to this integrated theory the provision of these necessary functions is the responsibility of leadership, although that does not imply that the leader will perform all of them himself or herself. Indeed, in groups over the size of about five members there are too many functions required for any one person to supply them all himself or herself.

Various attempts have been made to list the functions but they suffer from several disadvantages. In the first place, some researchers have produced three separate lists, one for each area. The difference between 'Task' and 'Team Maintenance' is always in danger of yawning into a dichotomy. The value of the three *overlapping* circles is that they emphasize the essential unity of leadership: a single action can be multi-functional in that it touches all three areas. The distinction between the circles should not therefore be pressed too far, and separate lists favour that unfortunate tendency. Secondly, many of the lists reflect the 'group dynamics laboratory' situation too much. Thirdly, it is rather artificial to categorize the response of leaders to individual needs. It is sufficient to recognize that effective leaders are aware of this dimension, and respond in appropriate ways with understanding. Such action might range from changing the content of an individual's job or role, along the lines advocated by Professor Herzberg, to a promotion or a word of encouragement.

It is perhaps best to work out a single list of leadership functions within the context of a given working situation, so that the sub-headings can have the stamp of reality upon them. But there is general agreement upon the essentials, and to illustrate some of these major functions meeting the three interacting areas of need, I give here a list originally worked out at the Royal Military Academy, Sandhurst, which has been the basis for numerous adaptations in industry and other fields:

- *Planning*
  Seeking all available information.
  Defining group task, purpose or goal.
  Making a workable plan (in right decision-making framework).

- *Initiating* eg briefing group on the aims and the plan.
  Explaining why aim or plan is necessary.
  Allocating tasks to group members.
  Setting group standards.

13

■ *Controlling*
Maintaining group standards.
Influencing tempo.
Ensuring all actions are taken towards objectives.
Keeping discussion relevant.
Prodding group to action/decision.

■ *Supporting*
Expressing acceptance of people and their contribution.
Encouraging group/individuals.
Disciplining group/individuals.
Creating team spirit.
Relieving tension with humour.
Reconciling disagreements or getting others to explore them.

■ *Informing*
Clarifying task and plan.
Giving new information to the group, ie keeping them 'in the picture'.
Receiving information from group.
Summarizing suggestions and ideas coherently.

■ *Evaluating*
Checking feasibility of an idea.
Testing the consequences of a proposed solution.
Evaluating group performance.
Helping the group to evaluate its own performance against standards.

SHARING DECISIONS

Without forgetting the broader opportunities open to members for supplementing the work of leadership in all three areas described above, it is especially useful to examine specifically the extent to which the leader should share with others the general function of *decision-making*, the core of such more definite functions as setting objectives and planning.

In an invaluable diagram R Tannenbaum and W H Schmidt[3] plotted the possibilities of participation. The diagram can be compared to a cake: at one end the leader has virtually all of it, and at the other the group has the lion's share. In terms of a transaction between a leader and an individual follower the continuum also illustrates the degrees of delegation that are possible in the context of a given decision.

There is much to be said for moving as far to the right of the continuum as possible, for the more that people share in decisions which directly affect them the more they are motivated to carry them out – provided they trust the integrity of the leader who is inviting them to participate in the decision. Yet factors in the *situation* (especially the nature of the task and the time available for the decision) and the *group* (especially the attitudes, knowledge, and experience of members) will naturally limit the extent to which the right-hand edge of the continuum can be approached. Other limiting factors may be present in the personality of the leader or the value system and philosophy of a particular organization, factors which cannot be described as natural or intrinsic in the same way as the situational or group constraints.

There are some groups and organizations whose *characteristic* working situations (as contrasted to the actual ones they may be in for 90 per cent of their time) are essentially crisis ones, where by definition time is short for decisions and the matter of life or death rests upon prompt decisions from one man, eg operating theatre teams, fire brigades, police forces, airline crews and military organizations. Yet such groups are not always in crisis situations, and for training purposes, if for no other reason, they need to explore the decision-making scale. Moreover, although it is not always possible to share decisions

Use of authority by the leader						Area of freedom for subordinates
Leader makes decision and announces it	Leader 'sells' decision	Leader presents ideas and invites questions	Leader presents tentative decision subject to change	Leader presents problem, gets suggestions, makes decision	Leader defines limits; asks group to make decision	Leader permits sub-ordinates to function within limits defined by superior

Figure 1.3 *A continuum of shared decisions*

over *ends* (ie goals, objectives, aims or purpose) it is usually possible to involve others more or less fully in *means* (ie methods, techniques, conditions, and plans).

Rather than engaging in the fruitless attempt to establish a particular spot or 'style' on the scale which is 'best' we should see the continuum as a sliding scale, or as a thermometer marked with boiling and freezing points.[4] Where the latter points fall on the scale will depend upon the characteristic working situation of the group or organization. There will be a difference, for example, between an earth-shifting gang of labourers constructing a motorway and a research group in an electronics or chemical firm.

CONCLUSION

We can now construct a general idea or integrated concept of a leader as a person with certain *qualities* of personality and character, which are appropriate to the general *situation* and supported by a degree of relevant technical knowledge and experience, who is able to provide the necessary *functions* to guide a group towards the further realization of its purpose, while maintaining and building its unity as a team; doing all this in the right ratio or proportion with the contributions of other members of the team. The length of this last sentence clearly precludes it from ever becoming a neat definition, but it is a framework for drawing together the major strands of research into the nature of leadership without exhausting the inherent mystery present in it as in all human relations.

KEY POINTS

▪ Working groups and organizations are always unique – each has its own *group personality* – but all share in common three areas of *need*: to achieve the common task, to be held together as a working unity, and the needs that individuals bring into the group by virtue of being embodied persons.

▪ A *want* is a need that has become conscious. Conscious or unconscious, our needs are closely linked with our motivation – *why* we do things. Two US psychologists, Maslow and Herzberg, offer maps of how our individual needs motivate us at work.

▪ In my philosophy, however, the Individual Needs circle, so important for motivation, overlaps with the Task and Team circles. It is an interactive model: each of the circles influences its two neighbours, and is in turn influenced by them.

▪ Therefore there are factors *outside* the individual – in the Task and Team – that will influence his or her motivation – for good or ill. We are not self-contained entities.

- In order for the three areas of need to be met certain key functions have to be performed, such as *planning, initiating* and *controlling*. They are the responsibility of the leader, but that doesn't mean to say the leader does them all. In groups of more than five there are too many functional acts required for one person to do.
- A wise leader will involve the team in decision-making as far as possible, for the more that people share in decisions that affect their working life *the more they are motivated to carry them out*.

Look well into yourself; there is a source which will always spring up if you will search there.

Marcus Aurelis

2

Action-Centred Leadership

Most of the changes we think we see in life are merely truths going in or out of fashion.

Robert Frost

The model at the core of Action-Centred Leadership (ACL) – the three overlapping circles of Task, Team and Individual – has become one of the most widely taught concepts in the world. Its simplicity, coupled with its proven track record as a basis for leadership training courses, commends it to management developers. Many now use it to integrate a number of other concepts, ideas and practices which can be grouped under the heading of 'the human side of enterprise'. The ACL model is now acknowledged to be the equivalent in this field to Einstein's General Theory of Relativity in physics. For it does identify the three main forces at work in working groups and organizations, and it charts (by way of a Venn diagram of the three circles) their main interrelationships with a degree of predictive accuracy.

This simplicity, however, is deceptive. True simplicity is different from the simplistic or superficial. Einstein's words warn us against such a reduction: 'Everything should be made as simple as possible, but not more simple' he once said.

As this book reveals, the three-circle model contains surprising depths of meaning to those who are willing to think and reflect about it. But it is a great mistake to reduce my original concept of ACL down to just the three circles, however central and pivotal they may be to the whole. Many books which reproduce the three circles, and many organizations that purport to teach ACL, do tend to pick out the three-circles diagram because it is so distinctive. But they then skate over, or leave out altogether, other ingredients in the original ACL complex of ideas which I regard as essential. This can lead to distortion.

Indeed the originality of ACL lay not in its parts but in their integration into a whole which is more than their parts and in the application of them to training. By being brought into a new relation with one another those parts have undergone varying degrees of transformation, which is inevitable in any creative work.

But they have not lost their identity. And it has been my habit to name the parts and discuss them when talking to professional audiences.

THE WIDER ACL FRAMEWORK

Let me now list for you the constituent parts of the wider ACL general theory, as a preface to commenting briefly upon some of them:

- Qualities Approach to Leadership.

- Situational Approach to Leadership.

- Group or Functional Approach to Leadership.

- Task, Group (or Team) and Individual Needs.

- The Theories of Maslow and Herzberg on motivation (in relation to the Individual Needs circle).

- The Three-Circles Model.

- How the circles – or areas of need – interact.

- Functions of Leadership.

- How far should leadership be shared? In the Task area, for example, how far should the leader share decisions? The Tannenbaum and Schmidt model.

- Drawing the threads together: the integrated functional (or ACL) concept of leadership.

- The Levels of Leadership – Team, Operational and Strategic.

Since the inception of ACL that framework has been constant. That is what I have taught, in season and out of season. But in the outside world the parts themselves (which were self-evidently not my own creations) have suffered varying changes. They have fallen from vogue or risen again as fashions change. Let us look at some of those changes as measured against the constant message of ACL.

THE QUALITIES APPROACH

The Qualities Approach, for example, was universally unpopular after the Second World War among management theorists and social psychologists. The idea that leadership might characterize one person rather than another, not least because he or she possessed leadership qualities, was then deeply unfashionable in the United States among social scientists (as they then liked to be called) for cultural reasons. The ACL general theory was virtually unique in those days in retaining it as a contributory source to our understanding of leadership.

The false assumptions latent in the US understanding of leadership were indeed challenged by a few individuals, notably William H Whyte in *The Organizational Man* (1955). A decade later A H Maslow visited several organizations in California and commented:

> What I smell here is again some of the democratic dogma and piety in which all people are equal and in which the conception of a factually strong person or natural leader or dominant person or superior intellect or superior decisiveness or whatever is bypassed because it makes everybody uncomfortable and because it seems to contradict the democratic philosophy (of course, it does *not* really contradict it).[1]

It took more than another decade before US behavioural scientists, such as Warren Bennis and Bernard Bass, backtracked to the Qualities Approach. Then a spate of books on leadership poured from the US presses discussing the qualities required in leaders. In a sense this change of heart was market-led. What happened? Reeling under fierce competition from Japanese companies, corporate United States began to look for better *leadership* from their chief executives. They needed someone with a sense of direction at the helm to guide them through the stormy waters of uncertainty. One or two US writers began to study the qualities of such leaders as

Lee Iacocca at Chrysler or Jack Welch of General Electric and suddenly the floodgates were opened and it was permissible once more in the United States to speak about leaders as unusual or gifted individuals.

In original ACL theory the first principle about the qualities of leaders suggests that they tend to possess (or should exemplify) the *qualities expected or admired in their work groups*. Physical courage, for example, does not make you into a military leader, but you cannot be one without it. A large part of the popularity of President Reagan, to give a second example, stemmed from the fact that many Americans saw him as personifying the core US characteristics and values. This point does suggest a powerful link between leadership and given work situations (such as engineering, nursing, or teaching), and may help to explain why the transfer of leadership from one field to another is often so difficult.

The British tradition on leadership has always emphasized the moral qualities of a good leader, such as moral courage and integrity. I cannot recollect ever talking about leadership without mentioning the importance of *integrity*. For, as Lord Slim said, integrity is the quality which makes people trust you. 'Trust being lost,' wrote the Roman historian Livy, 'all the social intercourse of men is brought to naught.'

From the beginning I also suggested that *enthusiasm* was a leadership quality, simply because I could not think of any leader I had met or read about who lacked it. Again, research over the last 30 years has amply confirmed that intuitive conclusion.

What I suggested at the end of the section on the Qualities Approach in my seminars was that you could – and should – go on thinking about the qualities of leadership for the rest of your life. There are always more facets of the diamond. Each leader you encounter may exhibit some particular quality or combination of qualities.

One particular methodological problem over qualities research has now been solved. The early US researchers compared some of the lists of qualities – such as initiative, perseverance, courage – which emerged from empirical research on leadership in order to see which words appeared on all or most lists. They found little or no agreement. For example, one classic survey of 20 experimental studies revealed that only 5 per cent of the leadership qualities examined were common to four or more studies. High intelligence came top; it appeared in 10 lists, followed by initiative which was mentioned in six of them. As there are some 17,000 words in the English language relating to personality and character there seemed to be plenty of choice and ample margin for error. These researchers were in fact victims of what philosophers have called the *word-concept fallacy*. Two words – such as *perseverance* and *persistence* – may be different, but they belong to the same family of meaning, the same concept. The researchers should have been fishing with wider meshed nets. For they should have been seeking clusters of meanings or concepts.

The mention of *integrity* on ACL courses has often provoked interesting discussions about the values of leadership. Was Hitler a good leader? How about Genghis Khan? What the research which went into my book *Great Leaders* (1989) has shown is that the English tradition concerning leadership (from whence sprang the US tradition) was fundamentally moral in complexion. Both the Graeco-Roman leadership tradition and the Biblical-Christian leadership tradition carried moral genes with them when grafted onto the existing tribal tradition of the nascent European nations. They held up the ideal of being a good leader and a leader for good. The same can be said for the great Chinese tradition of thought on leadership as exemplified by Confucius and Mencius.

It is true that a different message emanated from Machiavelli in the 16th century, but this godless Italian doctrine was never accepted into the mainstream of the Western tradition concerning leadership. The moral qualities approach – based upon Aristotle's four virtues: justice, prudence, fortitude and temperance – was far too deep-seated. Even in *The Path to Leadership* (1961) Field-Marshall Lord Montgomery could refer with approval to them. For this reason leaders in the Western culture who pursue immoral ends, or employ cynical, Machiavellian manipulation to achieve their ends, are unlikely to enjoy more than a brief success. Hitler did not last.

THE SITUATIONAL APPROACH

The situational approach, or contingency theory as it is now called, enjoyed a vogue in the 1960s mainly as a result of the work of Professor F E Fiedler of the University of Illinois and his associates. They studied the extent to which leadership veered towards the two poles of 'task oriented' and 'considerate' (or 'human relations') and tried to predict the circumstances in which one of these leadership 'styles' would be more effective than the other. Factors such as group composition, the degree of structuring in the task, and the 'position power' of the leader came into play. Fiedler believed that: 'We can improve the effectiveness of leadership by accurate diagnosis of the group-task situation and by altering the leader's work environment.'[2]

Like so many ideas and models, despite much revised work on the variables in the situation, Fiedler's work has not stood the test of time. It is now of little interest, except to specialists in the history of psychological research. But of course the idea that the influence of the situation pervades leadership is by no means out of date. ACL theory has always made four points under the heading of the Situational Approach:

- Situations are partly constant and partly variable. For example, working in a bank has a continuity and a uniqueness compared with, say, working in a hospital. This is true

25

of all fields, for they are all *unique*. But there has been much change in banking (as in all other fields). So it's a partly constant, partly changing situation.

■ Leaders personify or exemplify (or should do so) the qualities expected or required in their working groups. This principle clearly links leadership to particular working situations.

■ The Situational Approach highlights the importance of *knowledge* in leadership. There are three forms of authority in human affairs: the authorities of position, knowledge and personality. The latter in its extreme form is what is correctly called 'charisma'. Knowledge is especially important. As the proverb says, 'Authority flows to him who knows.' As I discovered in writing *Great Leaders*, it was Socrates who advanced for the first time the theory that knowledge was the key to the door of leadership.

■ Some people, however, who acquire considerable technical or professional knowledge, and are specialists in a particular kind of work, are not perceived by their colleagues or subordinates as leaders. In other words, there is more to leadership than technical knowledge. It is this more general or transferable aspect that the Qualities Approach attempted – with only partial success – to analyse and define.

In summarizing at the end of a talk on leadership I have usually made the point that a leader should possess knowledge, which will be partly technical or specialist and partly general. The more general leadership or management knowledge will include: an understanding of people and what motivates them; some knowledge of the Qualities, Situational and Functional Approaches to leadership; some knowledge of the process of effective thinking in its three applied forms – decision-making, problem-solving and creative thinking – so that one can guide a group in the process of making a decision, solving a problem or having new ideas; and, lastly, some knowledge about the principles and practice of good communication at interpersonal, group and organizational levels. Of course I am using 'knowledge' here to mean not only 'knowing about' in an academic sense of knowing facts, but the knowledge that can only be expressed in what you do and what you are.

Where does that leave us over the key issue of transfer? ACL theory suggests that a leader should have some degree of technical or professional knowledge. (That, incidentally, sets it apart from one popular version of the concept of management, which assumes that a manager once trained is equipped to manage in any kind of organization.)

It's a question of level really. At the *team* leadership level, technical or professional knowledge is clearly very important. Nobody is going to respect a leader who manifestly does not know what he or she is talking about. The 'leader' of an orchestra, for example, must be able to play the violin and lead the strings. At the *operational* and *strategic* levels of leadership, where the more general kinds of leadership knowledge become more important, the degree of technical or specialist knowledge required is smaller although none the less important. The conductor of an orchestra, to continue that example, does not have to be a good instrumentalist.

Transfer *within* a general field, such as industry or commerce, must be contrasted to transfer *between* general fields, such as military to politics, or industry to hospitals. Obviously the former is relatively more easy. A chief executive moving from company to company takes with him or her (or should do so) a transferable cluster of leadership skills – including decision-making and communication know-how – and also a transferable cluster of business abilities, notably in finance and marketing. All that remains to be learnt is the particular technology involved in the product or service. What matters now is speed of learning. A good strategic leader will soon acquire all that he or she needs to know. Lack of background knowledge can be turned into an advantage in so far as it keeps you out of the engine room when you should be on the bridge. Getting involved unnecessarily in detail is one of the failings of those who rise to the top in their own fields.

INDIVIDUAL NEEDS

As far as I know, Maslow did not himself actually use a diagram to illustrate his hierarchy of needs. The familiar model in the shape of a pyramid must therefore have been a later addition, but it is now commonplace in textbooks on management.

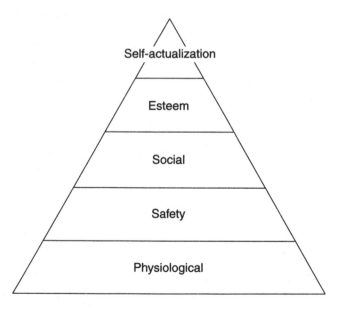

Figure 2.1 *The pyramid model of human needs*

Unfortunately this way of presenting Maslow's hierarchy makes it look as if our greatest needs are in the lower ranges, and that they narrow in size as you progress up the pyramid. But physiological needs, for example, are limited: you can only eat so many meals a day. In fact there are fewer limitations the further up you go. Therefore, it you persist with the pyramid model, it makes more sense to invert it thus:

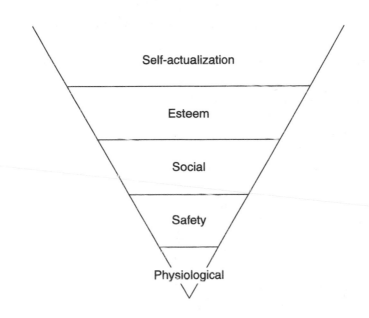

Figure 2.2 *The inverted pyramid of human needs*

I have left the diagram open-ended at the top in order to suggest that there may be another level of need beyond self-actualization, namely the need to transcend oneself. As we shall see later, Maslow virtually reached that important conclusion himself towards the end of his life.

Be that as it may, the visual difficulties of the pyramid in its original form are obviated if the diagram of boxes in ascending size (p. 10) is used. It has always seemed to me the better way of representing Maslow's hierarchy of needs.

LEADERSHIP AND MANAGEMENT FUNCTIONS

The list of leadership functions (see p. 13) originated as my synthesis of the *task* and *maintenance* functions taught in the US 'group dynamics laboratories' in the late 1950s. Apart from being in two lists instead of one the US compilations had the added disadvantage I have mentioned already, namely that they were redolent of the 'group laboratory' situation: leaderless groups with no other goal but 'to become a group' over a two-week period. As I was using the functional list as a basis for training real leaders in real situations the list had to be made generally applicable. For example, a function such as *summarizing* assumes importance in leading a discussiongroup, but it is a relatively minor skill if one is looking at the leadership functions required in a strategic leader.

The connection between the list that I produced from these sources and Henri Fayol's classic list of functions was soon noted.

Fayol, who was born in 1841, was a French mining engineer and became the director of a large group of coal pits before retiring in 1918. He published *General and Industrial Administration* two years earlier, but the first English translation of it did not appear until 1949. In it Fayol divided the activities of an industrial company into six main groups:

Technical   – production, manufacture, adaptation.

Commercial	– buying, selling, exchange.
Financial	– search for an optimum use of capital.
Security	– protection of property and people.
Accounting	– stocktaking, balance sheet, costs, statistics.
Administration	– forecasting and planning, organizing, commanding, co-ordinating and controling.

Fayol defined the function of command as 'getting the organization going' and he gives some examples of what it means in practice. A person in command should:

- Have a thorough knowledge of employees.

- Eliminate the incompetent.

- Be well versed in the agreements binding the business and its employees.

- Set a good example.

- Conduct periodic audits of the organization and use summarized charts to further this review.

- Bring together his chief assistants by means of conferences at which unity of direction and focusing of effort are provided for.

- Not become engrossed in detail.

- Aim at making unity, energy, initiative and loyalty prevail among all employees.

Fayol's analysis of managing in terms of functions has been subjected to much critical discussion. L F Urwick, an early British exponent of Fayol's theory, in his *The Elements of Administration* (1947), substituted the English word 'leadership' for Fayol's 'command'.

The ACL general theory provides a natural framework for Fayol's pioneering work. In it Fayol's list of functions could be developed in such a way as to ensure that all three areas of need – task, team or group, and individual – are met. It points out that a classic function such as *planning*, which may seem to be merely a task function, in fact influences both the other areas of need for good or ill. Moreover, Fayol is brought up to date by the addition of some more general functions in the team-building and team maintenance area, as well as functional responses to the individual needs circle.

THE DECISION-MAKING CONTINUUM

The Tannenbaum and Schmidt continuum, which first appeared in the *Harvard Business Review*, was always integral to the ACL general theory. It has a direct link with motivation for the reason given, namely that *the more that people share in a decision which affects their working life the more they tend to be motivated to carry it out*. This is a fundamental principle in motivation.

In the United States after 1960 (the date when I first encountered it there) the Tannenbaum and Schmidt chart slipped gradually into relative obscurity. The authors did produce a revised version of it in the *Harvard Business Review*, but their second thoughts obscured rather than enhanced the value of the original model.

In Britain the Tannenbaum and Schmidt continuum was the subject of academic research which has greatly enhanced its standing. It is now clear that people do expect leaders to be *consistent* in personality and character (for integrity suggests loyalty to standards outside oneself), yet *flexible* when it comes to decision-making. So that an effective leader, it has been shown, will make decisions on different points of the continuum during a single working day and be right each time. For he or she will be taking into account – consciously or subconsciously – such factors as the knowledge, motivation and experience of the group or individual concerned, the time available, whether or not issues of life-and-death are involved, and the values of the particular organization. No leader or manager gets it right every time, but training can help to cut down dramatically the number of times that inappropriate choices on the decision-making continuum are made.

THE LEVELS OF LEADERSHIP

Leadership exists on different levels. There is the team level, where the leader is in charge of 10 to 15 people. The operational leader is responsible for a significant part of the business, such as a business unit, division or key functional department. Invariably operational leaders have more than one team leader reporting to them.

At the strategic level, the leader, often the CEO, is leading the whole organization. 'Strategic leadership', a phrase I coined in 1970, is actually an expansion of the original, for in Greek, 'strategy' is made up of two words: 'stratos', a large body of people, and the '-egy' ending, which means leadership. Strategy is the art of leading a large body of people.

The key to achieving sustainable business success is to have excellence in leadership at all three levels. Strategic, operational and team leaders need to work harmoniously together as the organization's leadership team.

The three-circle model and the principles of leadership apply at all three levels, but obviously complexity increases the higher up you go. For the seven key functions of a strategic leader, see my *Effective Strategy in Leadership* (2002).

KEY POINTS

▪ Although the three-circle model and the linked functions of leadership form the centre of my practical philosophy, there are some important satellites: the Qualities and Situational Approaches, Maslow and Herzberg, the Decision-making Continuum, and the concept of the three levels of leadership.

▪ Enthusiasm, integrity, the combination of toughness or demandingness and fairness, humanity and warmth, humility (openness and lack of arrogance): these are some of the generic qualities of a good leader – and a leader for good.

▪ The Situational Approach highlights the influence of the characteristic working situation of a group or organization on who is chosen to occupy the role of leader. Technical or professional knowledge is a major strand in authority.

▪ Maslow's Hierarchy suggests some of the main needs that we have as individual human beings. Many of them are met in full or part by participating in working teams.

▪ The concept of leadership functions as set out in ACL is illuminated by comparing it with Henri Fayol's pioneering attempt at analysing management in functional terms. You can see what a difference it makes to have today's knowledge of the three circles.

- Decision-making can be shared by a leader with a team within the limits defined by the situation. This has important implications for motivation. For the more we share in decisions that affect our working life the more we tend to be motivated to implement them.

- Leadership exists at different levels – *team, operational* and *strategic*. The secret of having a highly motivated and top-performing organization is to have excellence in leadership at all levels.

- What I discovered, it is now generally recognized, is the universal or generic role of leader. That brought with it the immense practical benefit that we can now select and, given that the potential is there, train people to be leaders.

The lantern carrier should go ahead.

Japanese proverb

3

The Fifty-Fifty Rule

No man does anything from a single motive.
Samuel Taylor Coleridge

You may probably have come across the Pareto Principle in your study of management. The Pareto Principle, named after an Italian economist, states that the significant items of a given group form a relatively small part of the total. For example, 20 per cent of the sales forces will bring in 80 per cent of the business. As that ratio seems to hold true in many areas, it is often called the 80/20 rule or the concept of 'the vital few and trivial many'. I came across it in the context of time management: 80 per cent of your really productive and creative work will be done in 20 per cent of your time.

It occurred to me that a similar principle is at work in the field of motivation, which could be formulated thus:

> Fifty per cent of motivation comes from within a person and 50 per cent from his or her environment, especially from the leadership encountered there.

The Fifty-Fifty Rule in motivation does not claim to identify the different proportions in the equation exactly. It is more like a rough-and-ready rule of thumb. In effect is says no more than that a substantial part of motivation lies within a person while a substantial part lies, so to speak, outside and beyond control.

A child, for example, might have a potential interest in science and be generally ambitious to do well at school and go to university. But the Fifty-Fifty Rule comes into play. Fifty per cent of the child's progress will depend upon the academic quality of the school and in particular upon the personality and ability of the science teacher. A great schoolteacher has been defined as 'one whose actual lessons may be forgotten, but whose living enthusiasm is a quickening, animating and inspiring power'.[1]

The Fifty-Fifty Rule does have the benefit of reminding leaders that they have a key part to play – for good or ill – in the motivation of people at work. Fortunately (or unfortunately) not all the cards are in their hands, for they are dealing with people who are self-motivating in various degrees. The art of leadership is to work with the natural grain of the particular wood of humanity which comes to hand. Selection is important, for – in the blunt words of the Spanish proverb – 'You cannot carve rotten wood.'

I have set out the Fifty-Fifty Rule early in this book because you should bear it in mind when reading the theories of Maslow and Herzberg on motivation. Both of these men were professors of psychology in universities and both subscribed to an exceptionally individualistic philosophy. It is not too much of an exaggeration to say that their principle would be that 90 per cent of motivation lies within the individual.

Herzberg might have added that the environment and the supervision within it (he never used the word 'leadership') has power to *demotivate* or dissatisfy people, but he accorded managers no power to *motivate* them.

According to the ACL general theory, however, and the Fifty-Fifty Rule, both Maslow and Herzberg were overstating the case. Apart from our individual needs there are other needs emanating from the common task and the group or organization involved which have at least a potential motivational influence upon us. The value, worthwhileness or importance of the work we are doing, in the context of a changing and challenging environment, can enlist our deepest interest and engage our purposive energy. Leaders are often interpreters to us of the hidden values, needs and challenges of our daily work.

Contrary to the general tenor of Maslow and Herzberg, then, 50 per cent of our motivation lies without us. That does not, of course, mean that it is pointless to study the work of these two thinkers. Their contribution lies in the two sketchmaps they have given us of the *internal* needs and motivations that individuals bring with them into the working situation, and which are to some extent or other met by work.

Before Maslow and Herzberg it was of course known that individuals have needs which connect with motives. But what these two US thinkers contributed were sketchmaps of how these needs relate to one another. Maslow's sketchmap is more general and more original. Herzberg's sketchmap, however, has the merit of applying Maslow's thought to the industrial situation. Herzberg's dichotomy of human needs into satisfiers and dissatisfiers, or motivational and hygiene factors, has – as we shall see – some validity. But its chief merit is as a teaching device: if things are presented to us in terms of black-or-white even the most purblind will notice the difference, while a presentation in terms of various shades of grey may make little impact.

There is also a valuable teaching element in the Fifty-Fifty Rule. You may recall the old proverb, 'There are no bad soldiers, only bad officers.' Now as a statement this is not really true. There *are* bad soldiers. But it's a very good maximum to teach young officers, for it puts them on their mettle. It invites them to examine themselves and their own leadership before blaming the troops. Thus it inoculates them against one form of rationalization.

'Mutiny, Sir! Mutiny in my ship!' exclaimed Nelson's friend Admiral Collingwood when told that the complaints of some men amounted to mutiny. 'If it can have arrived at that, it must be my fault and the fault of every one of my officers.'

The same maxim applies to young or older managers. If there is an industrial strike how many chief executives and managers would begin like Collingwood by blaming themselves and questioning their collective leadership? 'If you are not part of the solution you are part of the problem.' The Fifty-Fifty Rule is an invitation to get your part in the motivational relationship right.

Doubtless, like the Pareto Principle, other applications of the Fifty-Fifty Rule will soon be discovered. As I have already mentioned in *Effective Teambuilding* (1986), it applies to the relative values of leadership and teamwork: 50 per cent of success depends on the team and 50 per cent on the leader. Again these are not scientific proportions. But they do indicate just how substantial is each contribution, regardless of that made by the other party. Here the Fifty-Fifty Rule challenges the leader (or team or individual team member) to get his or her part right first before criticizing the quality of contribution of the other party. It is the ultimate cure to the 'Us and Them' disease of organizations.

We could apply the same principle to the Nature versus Nurture debate. About half our destiny depends upon inherited characteristics or tendencies; the other half depends upon what we (or others) make of them. In the second part of that proposition lies the real challenge to parents and teachers. Certainly that applies in the leadership field. The idea that leaders are born and not made is a half truth. The full truth is that they are (about) half born and (more-or-less) half made – by experience and thought, by training and practice. This mixture of self-teaching and teaching by others of course takes a lifetime. For paradoxically it takes a long time to become a natural leader.

The Fifty-Fifty Rule ties in well with the meaning of the word 'motivation'. In fact it is a relatively new word, being introduced from the United States in the 1940s. Like the native English word 'motive' it can be used as a neutral explanation of cause: what *motivated* him to commit the murder? Or it can indicate a conscious desire or inculcate a desire for something or other: students *motivated* to learn by the encouragement of a good teacher.

The main US dictionary defines motivation in this second sense rather inaccurately as 'to provide with a motive', for the elements of motive energy can be there already. Motivation is closer in meaning to the older English concept of *motivity*: the power of initiating or producing movement. All these words – motive, motivation, motivity – come from the Latin verb 'to move'. What moves us to action may come from within or from without, or – more commonly – from some combination of inner impulse or proclivity on the one hand and outer situations or stimuli on the other.

The merit, then, of 'motivation' as a word is that it fits perfectly the Fifty-Fifty Rule. For it covers both what happens inside individuals in terms of wanting to do something and also what happens outside them as they are influenced by others or by circumstances. When someone is motivating you, he or she is consciously or unconsciously seeking to change the strength and/or direction of your motive energy.

This second aspect of motivation does raise an ethical issue. As I have suggested above, we are actually dependent in varying degrees upon outside stimulation of various kinds in all aspects of our mental life, not least our motivation. But this human dependency on others can be used for our own ends. How does legitimate influence differ from manipulation?

To manipulate someone means to control or play upon him or her by artful, unfair or insidious means, especially to one's own advantage. Therefore there are two aspects of manipulation: the means and the ends. If it is *your* purpose and not a *common* purpose that is being served, you are running into the danger of manipulation. If the means you employ to motivate others are hidden from them or seek to bypass their conscious minds, then one is becoming a manipulator rather than a motivator.

Motivating others, therefore, should not be confused with manipulatory practices used by strong personalities to dominate weaker ones. Leadership exists in its most natural form among equals. It is not the same as domination or the exercise of power. True leaders respect the integrity of others. Bosses demand respect; leaders give respect. Granted such a relationship, based upon mutual trust and supported by a common sense of justice or fairness, then it is part of the responsibility of leaders to stir up enthusiasm for the common task.

KEY POINTS

■ Maslow and Herzberg, the best-known theorists on motivation in the field of management studies, conceived motivation as an individual's response to an unfolding pattern of inner needs, ranging from food and safety to achievement and self-fulfilment. 'A satisfied need ceases to motivate,' said Maslow.

▦ Although there is truth in their theory it is wrong to see individuals in this atomistic way, for we are more like open systems than closed boxes.

▦ Both Maslow and Herzberg were driven by a set of humanistic values that made the self-realization of the individual the supreme good in life. They wanted work to serve that end, not frustrate it. They saw only one circle – Individual Needs. 'Job enrichment', the restructuring of jobs to allow for the higher needs to be met, was their answer to the problem of motivation. They had no concept of leadership.

▦ With the discovery of the three circles we now know where Maslow and Herzberg went wrong. The Task and the Team circles create needs as well as the Individual, and they are important ingredients in motivation.

▦ From the three circles stems the 50/50 Principle. Fifty per cent of our motivation comes from within us and 50 per cent from without us – from our environment, especially the people around us. (These proportions are indicative rather than mathematical; they may vary from person to person.)

▦ Within these critical 'external' factors the nature and quality of the leadership present is vitally important; hence the strong links between leadership and motivation.

When the best leader's work is done the people say, 'We did it ourselves!'

Lao-Tzu

PART 2

Maslow and Herzberg

4

Maslow's Hierarchy of Needs

Motives are generally unknown.

Samuel Johnson

Abraham Maslow died in 1970, having spent most of his long working life as lecturer and professor in psychology at Brandeis University in the State of New York. From an intellectual standpoint, Maslow's most formative years were those which he had spent in the late 1930s in New York, then, as he later declared, 'beyond a doubt, the centre of the psychological universe of that time.'[1] His preceding studies at the University of Wisconsin had included comparative and experimental psychology, biology and neurophysiology. In New York he concentrated upon the study of psycho-analysis under Erich Fromm, and he was himself analysed by Emil Oberholzer, which he judged to be 'the best learning experience of all'. But discussions with Alfred Adler not only introduced him to some of the shortcomings of the various forms of the Freudian theory, but also gave him a lasting sense that Adler's own contribution had been insufficiently appreciated by US psychologists.

Besides the analytical school, Maslow also studied the two other incipient schools in the contemporary psychology of his day, which he named respectively the 'holistic' and the 'cultural'. The word 'holism' (from the Greek word for whole) had been first introduced in 1926 by J C Smuts in his seminal book *Holism and Evolution* to describe 'the principle which makes for the origin and progress of wholes in the universe'.[2] Maslow learnt the application of the holistic approach to psychology from Max Wertheimer and Kurt Koffka, both prominent members of the Gestalt school. Later he believed that he had found a bridge between the holistic and analytic schools in the teachings of Kurt Goldstein, whose book *The Organism*, published in 1939, in particular exerted a profound and lifelong influence on Maslow.

Apart from investigating the social and cultural aspects of psychology, primarily with the aid of the anthropologist Ruth Benedict, Maslow also made a short field study of the Northern Blackfoot Indians. In addition, he had numerous conversations with other anthropologists in New York in the 1930s, such as Margaret Mead. But a list of his 19 publications in that decade shows that his own academic work was still experimental in orientation, and largely concerned with aspects of the behaviour of monkeys and apes. His interest in social anthropology does not appear to have gone very deep.

In 1954, Maslow (by then at Brandeis University) published a volume of articles and papers, of which all but five had been published in the preceding 13 years, under the title *Motivation and Personality*. Maslow had planned this collection in advance to be a synthesis of the analytical, *Gestalt* and social anthropological schools, feeling that they were 'intrinsically related to each other, and that they were subaspects of a single, larger, encompassing whole'. He also hoped that together they would help to make 'more meaningful' his earlier work in experimental psychology. 'Furthermore,' he added, 'I felt they would enable me to serve better my humanistic aims.'

'A Theory of Motivation', which appears as Chapter 5 in Maslow's book and has been quite the most influential paper in the volume so far, was first published as an article in the *Psychological Review* in 1943, and it has been reprinted many times since then. The major theme of the theory was announced in the preceding chapter, which was also published as a separate article in 1943:

> Man is a wanting animal and rarely reaches a state of complete satisfaction except for a short time. As one desire is satisfied, another pops up to take its place. When this is satisfied, still another comes into the foreground, etc. It is characteristic of the human being throughout his whole life that he is practically always desiring something. We are faced then with the necessity of studying the relationships of all the motivations to each other and we are concomitantly faced with the necessity of giving up the motivational units in isolation if we are to achieve the broad understanding that we seek for.

In 'A Theory of Motivation' which followed, Maslow sought to establish 'some sort of hierarchy of prepotency' in the realm of basic human needs, and to comment upon the difference this hierarchy would make to our understanding of motivation. He discussed these basic needs and their relationship to one another under five headings, which are now considered in turn.

THE PHYSIOLOGICAL NEEDS

The concept of physiological drives has usually been taken as the starting point for motivational theory. Maslow advocated the use of the word 'need' as an alternative to 'drive', basing his case on the notion of physical homeostasis, the body's natural effort to maintain a constant normal state of the blood-stream, coupled with the finding that appetites in the sense of preferential choices of good are a fairly efficient indicator of actual deficiencies in the body. Not all physiological needs were homeostatic, for the list could be extended to include sexual desire, sleepiness, sheer activity and maternal behaviour in animals. Indeed, if a growing loss of specificity in description were acceptable, he held that it would be possible to extend the list of physiological needs very considerably.

For two reasons Maslow considered the physical needs to be unique rather than typical of the basic human needs. First, they could be regarded as relatively independent of one another and other orders of need. Second, in the classic cases of hunger, thirst and sex, there was a localized physical base for the need. Yet this relative uniqueness could be be equated with isolation: the physiological needs might serve as channels for all sorts of other needs as well. The man who thinks he is hungry, for example, may be looking for security rather than carbohydrates or proteins.

If a man becomes chronically short of food and water he becomes dominated by the desire to eat and to drink, and his concern for other needs tends to be swept away. Thus the physiological needs are the most prepotent of all needs. What this prepotence means precisely is that the human being who is missing everything in life in an extreme fashion will still tend to seek satisfaction for his or her physiological needs rather than any others. Under such temporary dominance a person's whole attitude to the future may undergo change: 'For our chronically and extremely hungry man, Utopia can be defined simply as a place where there is plenty of food ... Such a man may fairly be said to live by bread alone.'

Supposing, however, a person has plenty of food guaranteed to him or her in the foreseeable future? Then, declared Maslow, another unsatisfied need emerges to dominate the organism. In other words, a satisfied want ceases to motivate. If a person has an endless supply of bread, at once other needs emerge and they supersede the physiological needs in dominating the organism. And when these in turn are satisfied, yet higher needs emerge, and so on. This is what Maslow meant by asserting that the basic human needs are organized into a hierarchy of relative prepotency.

Maslow entered an early caveat against a possible misinterpretation of his theory by advancing the hypothesis that individuals in whom a certain need had always been gratified would be the best equipped to tolerate a later frustration in that area. On the other hand, those who had been deprived would respond in a different way to eventual satisfaction than those who had been more fortunate in their younger days.

THE SAFETY NEEDS

When the physiological needs are relatively well satisfied, a new set of needs emerges centred upon the safety of the organism. Owing to the inhibition by adults of any signs of reaction to threat or danger this aspect of human behaviour is more easily observed in children, who react in a total manner to any sudden disturbance, such as being dropped, startled by loud noises, flashing lights, by rough handling, or by inadequate support.

Maslow found other indications for the need of safety in a child's preference for routine or rhythm, for a predictable and orderly world. Injustice, unfairness or lack of consistency in the parents seem to make a child feel anxious and unsafe. 'This attitude may be not so much because of the injustice *per se* or any particular pains involved; but rather because this treatment threatens to make the world look unreliable, or unsafe, or unpredictable.' The consensus of informed opinion held that children thrived best upon a *limited* permissiveness, for they need an organized or structured world. The sight of strange, unfamiliar or uncontrollable objects, illness or death can elicit fear responses in children. 'Particularly at such times, the child's frantic clinging to his parents is eloquent testimony to their role as protectors (quite apart from their roles as food givers and love givers).'

In adults we may observe expressions of the safety needs in the common desire for employment and with security of tenure, pension and insurance schemes, and the improvement of safety conditions at work. Another attempt to seek safety and stability in the world may be seen in the very common preference for familiar rather than unfamiliar things, or for the known rather than the unknown. Maslow added also the common suggestion that the appeal of religions and philosophies, which organize the universe and the people in it into some sort of coherent whole, may in part stem from this universal human need for safety and security.

Neurotic individuals may be characterized as adults who have retained their childish attitudes to the world. They perceive the world as hostile, overwhelming and threatening. Their urge towards safety or escape may take the form of a search for some strong all-powerful protector, or become a frantic effort to order the world so that no unexpected or unfamiliar dangers will ever appear. All sorts of ceremonials, rules and formulas might be employed so that every possible contingency is guarded against. Doubtless, however, Maslow would have allowed that rituals and rules could perform quite different functions for healthy or mature people.

THE SOCIAL NEEDS

If the physiological and safety needs are met, then the needs for love, affection and belongingness emerge as the dominant centre of motivation. The person concerned will feel keenly the absence of friends, wife or children; he will strive for affectionate relations with people and for 'a place in his group'.

Although Maslow distinguished between love and sex, and he showed an awareness that love needs to involve both giving and receiving love, it is an important characteristic of his psychology that he generally reserved the use of the word 'love' for close personal relationships. There is much to be said for following later practice and calling this set the 'Social Needs'.

THE ESTEEM NEEDS

This order includes both the need or desire for a high evaluation of self (self-respect or self-esteem) and for the esteem of others. Maslow divided them into two subsidiary sets:

■ the desire for strength, achievement, adequacy, mastery, competence, confidence in the face of the world, independence, and freedom; and

■ the desire for reputation, prestige, status, dominance, recognition, attention, importance and appreciation.

From theological discussions of *hubris* as well as from such sources as the writings of Eric Fromm, Maslow believed that:

we have been learning more and more of the dangers of basing self-esteem on the opinions of others rather than on real capacity, competence, and adequacy to the task. The most stable and therefore most healthy self-esteem is based on *deserved* respect from others rather than on external fame or celebrity and unwarranted adulation.

THE NEED FOR SELF-ACTUALIZATION

Even if all these needs are satisfied [wrote Maslow] we may still often (if not always) expect that a new discontent and restlessness will soon develop, unless the individual is doing what he is fitted for. A musician must make music, an artist must paint, a poet must write, if he is to be ultimately at peace with himself. What a man *can* be, he *must* be. This need we may call self-actualization.

This term, first coined by Kurt Goldstein, is being used in this book in a much more specific and limited fashion. It refers to man's desire for self-fulfilment, namely, to the tendency for him to become actualized in what he is potentially. This tendency might be phrased as the desire to become more and more what one is, to become everything that one is capable of becoming …

The clear emergence of these needs usually rests upon prior satisfaction of the physiological, safety, love and esteem needs.[2]

THE DESIRES TO KNOW AND UNDERSTAND

Maslow allowed that there were two other sets of needs which found no place in the above hierarchical order, and he felt it necessary to recognize them while make it clear that at present psychologists had little to say about them. He suggested, however, that the principle of a hierarchy of prepotency might also apply in both cases, albeit in a shadowy form. In contemporary presentations of Maslow's theory of needs in management education, these two scales are usually and unfortunately omitted altogether. It should be noted also that there is some ambiguity about Maslow's language at this point. When he wrote about 'higher needs' he is sometimes referring to esteem and self-actualization; at other times, however, he has in mind the cognitive and aesthetic needs described below.

Maslow began marshalling the evidence for such desires by noting the presence of 'something like human curiosity' in monkeys and apes. He continued:

> Studies of psychologically healthy people indicate that they are, as a defining characteristic, attracted to the mysterious, to the unknown, to the chaotic, unorganized, and unexplained. This seems to be a *per se* attractiveness; these areas are in themselves and of their own right interesting. The contrasting reaction to the well-known is one of boredom.

The gratification of the cognitive impulses is subjectively satisfying. Moreover,

> even after we know, we are impelled to know more and more minutely and microscopically on the one hand, and on the other, more and more extensively in the direction of a world philosophy, theology etc. The facts that we acquire, if they are isolated or atomistic, inevitably get theorized about, and either analysed or organized or both. This process has been phrased by some as the search for meaning. We shall then postulate a desire to understand, to systematize, to organize,

to analyse, to look for relations and meanings, to construct a system of values.

Maslow concluded with a warning against making a too sharp dichotomy between the cognitive and the conative (or basic needs) hierarchies.

THE AESTHETIC NEEDS

Maslow was convinced that:

> in *some* individuals there is a truly basic aesthetic need. They get sick (in special ways) from ugliness, and are cured by beautiful surroundings; they *crave* actively, and their cravings can be satisfied *only* by beauty. It is seen almost universally in healthy children. Some evidence of such as impulse is found in every culture and in every age as far back as the cavemen.

The conative, cognitive and aesthetic needs overlap so much that it is impossible to separate them sharply.

> The needs for order, for symmetry, for closure, for completion of the art, for system, and for structure may be indiscriminately assigned *either* to cognitive, conative, or aesthetic, or even to neurotic needs.

COPING AND EXPRESSIVE BEHAVIOUR

Lastly, Maslow expounded a useful distinction between coping (functional striving, purposive goal seeking) and expressive behaviour which does not try to do anything: 'it is simply a reflection of the personality'. As examples of expressive or non-functional behaviour, Maslow listed 'the random movements of a healthy child, the smile on the face of a happy man even when he is alone, the springiness of the healthy man's walk, and the erectness of his carriage'. Moreover, the *style* in which a person behaves may or may not be expressive. Yet even here Maslow warned against a false dichotomy: 'It is finally necessary to stress that expressiveness of behaviour and goal-directedness of behaviour are not mutually exclusive categories. Average behaviour is usually both.'

KEY POINTS

▪ Maslow's classification of needs into five categories – Physiological, Safety, Social, Esteem and Self-actualization – is a useful sketchmap for a practical leader. It is an aid to understanding human nature.

▪ The more basic needs are stronger, so that when they are threatened we jump back down the ladder and defend. The higher needs are weaker, but they are what make us distinctively human.

▪ The 'higher needs', according to Maslow, included not only the need to fulfil ourselves but also cognitive and aesthetic needs – the need to know and to understand. We need truth as well as beauty in our lives.

▪ Maslow's distinction between *coping* and *expressive* behaviour reflects a seminal insight. An artist is often highly motivated, but as his or her work is a form of self-expression it doesn't *feel* like work. A picture of motivation that sees humans as merely moved to achieve goals in response to external rewards or punishments, like mice in a cage, is a defective one.

No one really knows about other human beings. The best you can do is to suppose that others are like yourself.

John Steinbeck

5

The Application of Maslow's Ideas in Industry

All that we do is done with an eye to something else.

Aristotle

Maslow spent his working life as an academic psychologist. The relatively slight impact that his theory of a hierarchy of needs made upon other academic psychologists and psychiatrists can be explained partly by the internal state of those disciplines in the period of Maslow's lifetime, dominated as they had been by the Freudian and behaviourist orthodoxies. Among those psychologists who have specifically investigated human motivation in work, some have dismissed the theory simply as an unfounded hypothesis, while others have given it a guarded acceptance. There is some measure of agreement that the lower needs (physiological, safety and social) are organized into a hierarchy of prepotence, but less agreement that their satisfaction necessarily leads on to the experience of esteem and self-actualization needs.[1]

It is true that Maslow did occasionally make it clear that he did not regard progression up the hierarchy by means of satisfaction as an inevitable or inexorable process, but he did give the general impression that this was his underlying assumption about human nature, all things being equal. Yet it would be extremely hard, for example, to demonstrate any inherent progression from the esteem needs to the need for self-actualization. But apart from these doubts about the connections between lower and higher needs, those academic psychologists and psychiatrists who have read Maslow have received this theory with cautious but unmistakable interest as a stimulating if puzzling contribution to our knowledge of man.

DOUGLAS MCGREGOR'S THEORY X AND THEORY Y

This very slow growth of interest in the academic world must be contrasted with the rapid dissemination of Maslow's ideas in industry. The person mainly responsible for this work of popularization was the late Professor Douglas McGregor. Born in Detroit in 1906, the son of a Presbyterian minister, McGregor graduated at Wayne University and worked as a social psychologist at Harvard University before becoming a professor at the Massachusetts Institute of Technology. As a management consultant he worked with Standard Oil of New Jersey, Bell Telephone, Union Carbide and Imperial Chemical Industries (UK). He had a spell of six years as President of Antioch College in Ohio but returned to MIT. He was killed in a car accident in 1962.

Two years before his death, McGregor published his most influential book, *The Human Side of Enterprise*. In the early chapters he demonstrated with considerable clarity that the assumptions which managers make about human behaviour and human nature have a profound effect upon the way they seek to manage. Apart from his readable style, unusually free from jargon, McGregor's clarity stemmed from the fact that he polarized these assumptions into two clusters of propositions or theses about human nature, which he called Theory X and Theory Y.[2] Leaving out his explanatory glosses, we can set them out as follows:

Theory X: The Traditional View of Direction and Control

1. The average human being has an inherent dislike of work and will avoid it if he or she can.

2. Because of this human characteristic dislike of work, most people must be coerced, controlled, directed, threatened with punishment to get them to put forth adequate effort toward the achievement of organizational objectives.

3. The average human being prefers to be directed, wishes to avoid responsibility, has relatively little ambition, and wants security above all.

Theory Y: The Integration of Individual and Organizational Goals

1. The expenditure of physical and mental effort in work is as natural as play or rest.

2. External control and the threat of punishment are not the only means for bringing about effort toward organizational objectives. People will exercise self-direction and

self-control in the service of objectives to which they are committed.

3. Commitment to objectives is a function of the rewards associated with their achievement.

4. The average human being learns, under proper conditions, not only to accept but to seek responsibility.

5. The capacity to exercise a relatively high degree of imagination, ingenuity and creativity in the solution of organizational problems is widely, not narrowly, distributed in the population.

6. Under the conditions of modern industrial life, the intellectual potentialities of the average human being are only partially utilized.

Now McGregor has drawn heavily upon the work of Maslow: indeed, if one subtracts the Maslow-inspired passages there is not much left of Theory Y. McGregor had swallowed Maslow's theory of a hierarchy of needs hook, line and sinker, but he digested it into language which industrial and commercial managers could understand. Moreover, he integrated the theory with the more traditional preoccupations of management by suggesting that the needs of the individual and the needs of the organization were not inherently incompatible. Under the third proposition above in the Theory Y cluster, for example, McGregor commented: 'The most significant of such rewards, eg the satisfaction of ego and self-actualization needs, can be direct products of efforts directed towards organizational needs.'

If Theory Y rested upon optimistic assumptions about people buttressed by the writings of Maslow, Theory X, by contrast, had a darker foundation. In company with many other behavioural scientists before and since McGregor advanced for the justification of Theory X what could be called a modern management myth about the Genesis myth. The deepest roots of Theory X go down to the Garden of Eden. 'The punishment of Adam and Eve for eating the fruit of the Tree of Knowledge was to be banished from Eden into a world where they had to work for a living.' Obviously, McGregor supposed that this myth lay behind the assumption that a person has an inherent tendency to avoid work. Without doubting that pessimistic views of people both exist and exert influence upon human relationships, we may legitimately question how far these can be blamed upon such external sources as the Book of Genesis.

THE WIDER DISSEMINATION OF MASLOW'S IDEAS

McGregor's writings, still ranked as the most influential of their *genre* in the world of industry, and his persuasive lectures were not the only means by which Maslow's views have been propagated to management audiences. His disciples included such prominent behavioural scientists as Rensis Likert and Chris Argyris. Likert, as Director of the Institute for Social Research at Michigan University, studied the effects of different supervisors on the productivity of those who work under them, and found a significant correlation between high production and supervision which helped operatives to do the job well for their own satisfaction as much as for the attainment of departmental goals.[3] Argyris, as Professor of Industrial Administration at Yale University, tended to stress the element of conflict between the individual's and the organization's respective needs for self-actualization, but he added his powerful voice to the chorus advocating practical steps – such as 'job enlargement' and participation in problem solving and decision-making – for reconciling the two sets of goals.[4]

Maslow's theory also attracted the attention of sociologists as well as social psychologists. For example, in a study of the attitudes to work of 229 manual workers in Luton factories (Vauxhall, Skefko Ball Bearings, and Laporte Chemicals) J H Goldthorpe and his colleagues accepted that attempts to specify the range and structure of a hierarchy of human needs along the lines of Maslow might be both legitimate and relevant, but they expressed doubts as to whether or not one could make easy deductions about these general statements to particular cases.

There were particular sociological factors behind what they called the Luton workers' largely 'instrumental' attitude to their work – looking upon it as an instrument or means towards relatively high wages:

> For wants and expectations are culturally determined *variables*, not psychological constants; and from a sociological standpoint what is in fact of major interest *is* the variation in the ways in which groups differently located in the social structure actually experience and attempt to meet the needs which at a different level of analysis may be attributed to them all.[5]

To social factors we must add such personal variables as parental upbringing.[6] Moreover, where people are in their life cycle has some influence on what needs are dominant in their experience as motivating forces.

Goldthorpe's conclusion matched that of John Mason Brown. Writing in *Esquire* he said: 'Most people spend most of their days doing what they do not want to do in order to earn the right, at times, to do what they may desire.'

THE MORAL ISSUE

For at least some sociologists the discrepancy between Maslow's description of human nature and the lack of desire for self-actualization in some working environments has raised a moral issue. What place *ought* work to occupy in human life, quite apart from the role it may play in such loaded settings as the Luton factories? What changes – if any – in the social and cultural *milieu* should be encouraged, and why? The British industrial sociologist Alan Fox posed the issue in the following way:

> The broadest division is between those doctrines which seek to persuade us that work ought to be a central integrating principle of man's individual and social being, offering opportunities of choice, decision, and responsibility, and those who find no ethical difficulty in seeing its major significance in terms of its extrinsic outcome.[7]

Thus the application of Maslow's theory of a hierarchy of human needs to the task of understanding attitudes and behaviour at work in industry has already raised some fundamental moral questions about the place of work in life. But this is a secondary debate, albeit an important one. For even those who reject the liberal demand that work should now be so arranged as to allow maximum satisfaction possible in all five areas of individual need would accept that work should provide at least the financial means for pursuing the all-important goal of self-actualization outside the factory or the office, namely in leisure activities and family life. Either way the psychology of self-fulfilment as exemplified by Maslow's theory of needs marches on.

In the following chapter I shall consider the theory, researches and assumptions of Frederick Herzberg. There are two main reasons for doing so. The first reason is that Herzberg both offered what purports to be an alternative theory to that of Maslow and also claimed that evidence gathered by empirical methods proves this theory to be true. A second reason is that it keeps us in touch with the practical concerns of industry. For Herzberg was a leading exponent of that school which holds that work should play a central and integral (rather than instrumental) part in the process of healthy self-actualization, not simply for the few but for the many employed in industry, commerce and the public services.

KEY POINTS

- Maslow's most influential disciple in the field of management thought was Douglas McGregor. He showed that the assumptions, often unconscious, which managers make about human nature have a deep influence on how they actually treat people. He polarized these assumptions into Theory X and Theory Y.

- McGregor also expressed confidence that 'satisfaction of ego and self-actualization needs' can be reconciled with organizational needs. The three-circle model further clarifies the situation: there is indeed an overlap between task and individual needs, so that meeting one entails meeting the other. But there is also a tension between them. In some circumstances, for example, an individual may choose to sacrifice one or more of his or her own needs in order that the common purpose should be better served.

- True leaders do hold something like the Theory Y doctrine of human nature. They treat people *as if* they are great. Occasionally, of course, they will be let down, but they accept that as part of the price of leading. More often than not, people respond positively to trust: they *become* great.

Nobody inspires you more than the person who speaks to the greatness within you.

The task of leadership is not to put greatness in to people but to elicit it, for the greatness is there already.

John Buchan

6

Herzberg's Motivation – Hygiene Theory

Work is not the curse, but drudgery is.
Henry Ward Beecher

In 1959 Frederick Herzberg published his research into job attitudes in a book entitled *The Motivation to Work*. At the time of writing Herzberg, later Professor of Psychology at Western Reserve University, was Research Director at the Psychological Service of Pittsburgh. His co-authors, Bernard Mausner and Barbara Snyderman, were respectively Research Psychologist and Research Associate at the same institute.

With two other psychologists Herzberg and Mausner had carried out an earlier preliminary survey of the existing literature on the factors involved in attitudes to work.[1] Despite differences in content and methods in the 155 books and articles they considered, Herzberg and his colleagues felt able to draw a major conclusion:

> The one dramatic finding that emerged in our review of this literature was the fact that there was a difference in the primacy of factors, depending upon whether the investigator was looking for things the worker liked about his job or things he disliked. The concept that there were some factors that were 'satisfiers' and others that were 'dissatisfiers' was suggested by this finding. From it was derived one of the basic hypotheses of our own study.

BASIC CHARACTERISTICS OF THE RESEARCH PROJECT

After two pilot schemes, involving respectively 13 labourers, clerical workers, foremen, plant engineers and accountants, and 39 middle-managers (all but six of them engineers of one kind or another), the research team launched into a study of the job attitudes of 203 engineers and accountants working in nine factories of plants around Pittsburgh. The description and discussion of this particular research project formed the main content of *The Motivation to Work*; moreover, the methodology of the research served as a model for many replications in the next decade. Consequently it is important to grasp the essential methodological characteristics of the research Herzberg and his colleagues undertook. Owing to the style of the writers this is not always an easy task, but we can distinguish three major characteristics.

1. Specification of Experience

Each of the 203 subjects was asked to identify periods in his own history when his feelings about his job were markedly either higher or lower than usual. The researcher made the assumption that the respondents would be able to recognize the extremes of this continuum of feelings and to select extreme situations to report. They distinguished between short and long-term sequences of events, but in each case the 'story' had to be finite in terms of having a beginning, middle and end.

2. Factors-Attitudes-Effects

The research aimed at unravelling the interrelations between objective 'events' in the historical accounts, coupled with the feelings which were expressed about them by the subjects, and the effects which resulted. Rather confusingly, the reported events were labelled 'first-level factors' and the allied feelings 'second-level factors', while the word 'factor' was also used about the combination of both together. The word 'attitude' means in this context the more settled or habitual mode of regarding aspects of life. 'Effects' included job performance (based on the subject's own reports of quantifiable or qualitative changes), mental health, interpersonal relationships, attitude towards the company and other attitudes allied to the working situation.

3. Research Methods

The researchers employed the technique of the 'semi-structured' interview, in which the interviewer asks some pre-arranged questions but has freedom to pursue any lines of inquiry that he judges might be fruitful. 'The questions were so designed that for each story we were sure to get the factors-attitudes-effects information which we sought.' Each respondent could choose a story about a time when he felt exceptionally good or exceptionally bad about the job. After this sequence had been thoroughly discussed and analysed, the interviewer asked for a second story, which had to be opposite in terms of good/bad and short/long-range sequence of events from the first one. Some respondents volunteered a third or fourth story.

The researchers attempted to set up categories of factors and effects from the material gathered. Carefully cross-checking one another's judgments, the team broke down the replies into 'thought units', which was defined as 'a statement about a single event or condition that led to a feeling, a single characterization of a feeling, or a description of a single effect', eg the statement 'The way it was given to me showed the supervisor had confidence in my work.' A sample of 5,000 'thought units' of the entire (unspecified) total was sorted out into three major categories: first-level factors, second-level factors and effects. Each of these main ones was further sub-divided into lesser categories. Once 95 per cent agreement among them on the categories had been achieved, the research team proceeded to analyse 476 stories or 'sequences of events'.

THE CATEGORIES

Under the heading of 'First-level factors' the authors listed 14 categories of elements or acts in the situation which the respondents found to be sources of good or bad feelings, with the criteria which they had used to establish them.

1. *Recognition.* Any act of recognition, be it notice, praise or criticism ('negative recognition') served as the main criterion. The sub-categories allowed distinction between situations when concrete awards were given along with the acts of recognition and those in which they were not.

2. *Achievement*. Stories mentioning some specific success (or failure) were placed in this category, eg successful completion of a job, solutions to problems, vindication, and seeing the results of one's work.

3. *Possibility of growth*. Respondents mentioned changes in their situations involving objective evidence that the possibilities for professional growth had increased or decreased. Besides new vistas opened up by promotion this category included reports of increased opportunities in the existing situation for learning and practising new skills, or acquiring new professional knowledge.

4. *Advancement*. 'This category was used only when there was an actual change in the status or position of the person in the company.'

5. *Salary*. 'This category included all sequences of events in which compensation plays a role. Surprisingly enough, virtually all of these involve wage or salary increases, or unfulfilled expectation of salary increases.'

6. *Interpersonal relations*. Under this general heading actual verbalizations about the characteristics of the interaction between the respondent and some other individual were divided into three categories according to the identity of the latter: superior, subordinate and peers. These were interactions which might take place in working hours but were independent of the activities of the job.

7. *Supervision-technical*. This category included remarks about the competence or incompetence, fairness or unfairness of the supervisor or superior. Comments upon the superior's willingness to delegate or teach, on his tendency to nag or perpetually criticize, would be classified under 'supervision-technical'.

8. *Responsibility*. This category covered those sequences of events in which the respondent mentioned satisfaction gained from being given (or denied) responsibility.

In cases, however, in which the story revolved around a wide gap between a person's authority and the authority he needed to carry out his job responsibilities the factor identified was 'company policy and administration'. The rationale for this was that such a discrepancy between authority and job responsibilities would be considered evidence of poor management.

9. *Company policy and administration*. This category included descriptions of adequate or inadequate organization and management. Apart from such structural components, remarks about the overall characteristics of the company's policy (especially its personnel policy) as harmful or beneficial were placed under this heading.

10. *Working conditions*. Comments about the physical conditions of work, the amount of work, facilities available, ventilation, tools, space and other environmental aspects came into this class of 'thought units'.

11. *Work itself*. Mentions of the actual doing of the job, or phases of it, as sources of satisfaction or dissatisfaction found places in this category.

12. *Factors in personal life*. This factor covered a range of statements about cases in which work impinged upon personal life in such a way that the effect was an ingredient in the respondent's feelings about his job. Family needs for salary levels or problems stemming from job location would be examples of this type of comment.

13. *Status*. This term was employed to classify any actual mentions of signs or appurtenances of status as being

constituents in reaction to the job, eg a secretary, company car, a certain eating facility.

14. *Job security*. Objective signs of the presence or absence of job security, such as tenure and company stability or instability, were listed under this factor.

Under the heading of 'Second-level factors' the researchers analysed the responses of the interviewee to the question, 'What did these events mean to you?' Naturally the information at this point was limited by the extent to which the respondents could articulate their feelings and the level of insight which enabled them to report real perceptions rather than stereotyped reactions based on socially accepted ideas. These second-level inferences or generalizations were therefore to be distinguished from the statements of feeling in the verbal responses of the first-level factors. The 11 second-level factors or clusters of feelings share for the most part the same names as the first-level ones; for example: recognition, achievement, possible growth, responsibility, belonging and interest. 'Feelings about salary' was included to cover those situations in which:

> the first-level factor was viewed primarily as a source of the things that money can bring. If an answer to the question, 'Why did this promotion make you feel good?' was, 'I like the idea of being able to make more money', then the second-level factor was coded 'salary'.

The analysis of *effects* into categories posed fewer problems, because most respondents were specific and concrete in their replies.

1. *Performance effects*. This major category included three sub-categories. The first consisted of general comments about work being better or worse than usual; the second

embraced comments about the rate of work; and in the third were mustered remarks concerning the quality of work.

2. *Turnover*. At one end of the 'turnover' continuum the respondent actually resigned or left his job; at the other his positive feelings about his work and the company had mounted so considerably that he turned down attractive offers to go elsewhere.

3. *Mental health effects*. Positive statements included a lessening of tension symptoms, gaining weight when underweight, and stopping too much drinking or smoking. The more numerous negative reports, however, mentioned psychomatic effects (skin disorders, ulcers, heart conditions), physiological changes related to tensions (such as severe headaches and loss of appetite), and more diffuse symptoms of anxiety possibly related to temperamental dispositions in the individual.

4. *Effects on interpersonal relationships*. There were many instances where the job had appeared to influence for better or worse a man's relationships with his family.

5. *Additional effects*. Respondents also reported changed attitudes towards themselves, their colleagues, their professions or the companies which employed them.

EXPERIMENTAL RESULTS

The major question that the research team had posed themselves was whether or not different kinds of factors brought about job satisfaction and job dissatisfaction. A number of minor questions which interested them related to the correlations between the variables of long-term and short-term sequences, first-level and second-level factors, effects and attitudes, profession, education, job level and experience. Broadly speaking, the team felt convinced that their main hypothesis that there *were* two distinct sets of factors involved had been justified by the study.

The factors that are rarely instrumental in bringing about high job attitudes focus not on the job itself but rather on the characteristics of the context in which the job is done: working conditions, inter-personal relationships, supervision, company policies, administration of these policies, effects on the worker's personal life, job security, and salary. This is a basic distinction. The satisfiers relate to the *actual job*. Those factors that do not act as satisfiers describe the *job situation*.

Heading the list of short-term 'satisfiers' in the first-level factors are *achievement* and *recognition*, followed by *work itself*, *responsibility*, *advancement* and the *possibility of growth*. In the second-level area the *possibility of growth* appeared with great frequency in the 'high satisfaction' stories. By reviewing all the variables the team suggested that the complex or cluster of achievement-recognition-responsibility-work itself-advancement are higher interrelated in both the short and long terms. 'When some or all of the factors are present in the job situation of an individual, the fulfilment of his basic needs is such that he enters a period of exceptionally positive feelings about his job.' For situational, professional or personal reasons the relative strengths of factors may vary, but the complex as a whole will always characterize job satisfaction.

Visually the discontinuity between the 'satisfiers' and 'dissatisfiers' and their relative longevity can be shown by means of a diagram:

As indicated in the legend of this figure, the distance from the neutral area shows the percentage frequency with which each factor occurred in the high job-attitude sequences and in the low job-attitude sequences. The width of the boxes represents the ratio of long-range to short-range attitude effects; the wider the box, the more frequently this factor led to a long-range job attitude change. The factors of recognition and achievement are shaded in this figure to indicate that the width of their boxes portrays a reversal in the long-range ratio. The attitude effects of both of these factors were substantially more short range.

The frequency and duration of *work itself, responsibility* and *advancement* suggest that they form the major strands of high job attitudes. They appear much less frequently in stories of times when the respondents felt unhappy with their job. These motivating factors focused on the job itself; the 'dissatisfiers' are concerned with the context of environment of the job. Salary has a short-term satisfying effect, but as an influence on job attitudes the research team concluded that it had more potency as a dissatisfier than as a satisfier. In the 'low' stories money tended to reflect a perceived unfairness in the wages policy or system of the company; in the 'high' stories it accompanied achievement: 'it meant more than money; it meant a job well done; it meant that the individual was progressing in his work.'

From their analysis of the 'second-level' factors, Herzberg and his colleagues concluded that:

a sense of personal growth and of self-actualization is the key to an understanding of positive feelings about the job. We would define the first-level factors of achievement-responsibility-work itself-advancement as a complex of factors leading to this sense of personal growth and self-actualization. In a later discussion we postulate a basic need for these goals as a central phenomenon in understanding job attitudes.

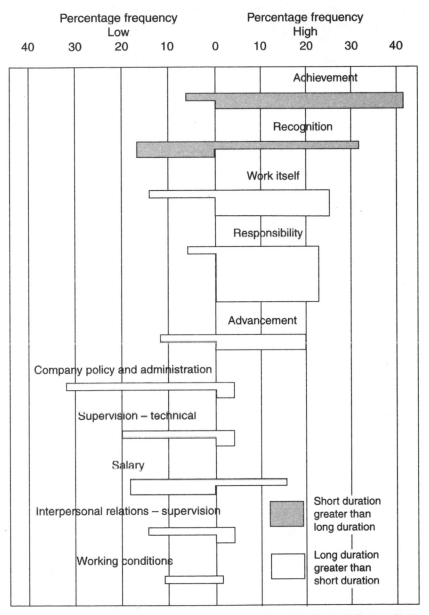

Figure 6.1 *Comparison of satisfiers and dissatisfiers (203 Pittsburgh engineers and accountants).*

Short-term positive feelings can then be regarded as 'partial reinforcements' of these basic needs.

For the complex of factors which describe the *surrounds* of the job and can cause discontent Herzberg recruited the word *hygiene* from the medical world.

> Hygiene operates to remove health hazards from the environment of man. It is not a curative; it is, rather, a preventive. Modern garbage disposal, water purification, and air-pollution do not cure diseases, but without them we would have more diseases.[5]

The 'satisfier' Herzberg and his associates named *motivators*. The former they linked with the 'avoidance needs', or the human tendency to avoid painful or unpleasant situations; the latter they connected directly with the concept that man's 'ultimate goal' is self-actualization or self-realization. In the work situation this general basic need finds a degree of fulfilment if the job allows some meeting of the related needs for professional growth and for the exercise of creativity. If these possibilities are intrinsically absent from the job, then heavy compensations in terms of hygiene factors would be necessary to adjust the balance. 'The motivators fit the need for creativity, the hygiene factors satisfy the need for fair treatment, and it is thus that the appropriate incentive must be present to achieve the desired job attitude and job performance.'

HERZBERG AND MASLOW

How does Herzberg's motivator-hygiene theory relate to Maslow's theory of a hierarchy of needs? Clearly they share in common the concept of self-actualization, derived from the writings of psychologists such as Jung and Adler. Herzberg's discussion of Maslow's theory in *The Motivation to Work* is both brief and unsatisfactory. The aspect of the theory which he seems to have felt unacceptable was the notion that the predominant needs of individuals might change and develop, rather than being seen as relatively fixed and immutable. Yet although Herzberg pressed home his distinction between the 'motivators' and 'hygiene', he himself allowed for some possibility of a fluctuating 'need hierarchy' operating within the two clusters, just as he left open the question as to whether different degrees of potency among the factors in the two sets would reflect different patterns of psychological characteristics in professional groups or individuals.

In contrast to the predominantly holistic bias of Maslow's mind, Herzberg's approach exhibits a dichotomizing tendency towards either/or and black-or-white thinking. It is possible that the opposite ends or poles of continuums in human behaviour may appear to take on a qualitative difference. By documenting such a phenomenon in relation to work Herzberg indirectly drew attention to the differing characteristics of Maslow's basic needs'. Psychological, safety and social needs, for example, might create dissatisfaction if they were not met, but they had little power to afford satisfaction. By contrast, the meeting of esteem and self-actualization needs could lead to a more positive and longer-lasting sense of satisfaction. On the other hand, the absence of a potential for self-actualizing progress might not create conscious dissatisfaction. Thus it could be said that Herzberg was only developing the hint in Maslow that the physiological needs form a poor model for the 'higher' needs in the hierarchy.[2] Moreover, Herzberg accepted the possibility, pending further research, that an individual's internal rating of 'satisfiers' and 'dissatisfiers' might reflect his or her personality development, ie presumably his or her progress in gratifying the hierarchy of basic needs. It is clear also that some psychologists (like some theologians and philosophers) have a temperamental bias towards dichotomizing, while others have predominantly holistic or synthetic minds.[3] Herzberg belongs to the first group, Maslow to the second. Allowing for the application to the work situation in particular and also the respective intellectual biases of the two psychologists, it may be concluded that the similarities between the approaches of Maslow and Herzberg outweigh their dissimilarities.[4]

Herzberg's general view that 'supervision' (he never called it leadership) is a hygiene factor obstinately ignores the fact that in many circumstances human relationships are as much intrinsic to the job as they are extrinsic. His attempt to distinguish between *interpersonal relationships* and *supervision-technical* does not alter his under-estimation of the satisfying or motivating influence of good leadership, both for the leader himself or herself and for those working with him or her.

Herzberg had a curiously rigid idea about management. The idea that leaders at all levels might be aware and respond to the needs of those working under them does not seem to have occurred to him at all. A stress on the vital importance of good leadership to ensure achievement and recognition, the delegation of responsibility and the provision of challenging tasks, finds no place in his writings, although he did allow that better supervision would be required if jobs were to be made more intrinsically satisfying. In other words, Herzberg may well have reacted so vigorously against the 'human relations' approach to management, personified by the growth of 'group sensitivity training', that he threw out the baby with the bath water.

This thesis may be supported by Herzberg's cavalier treatment of the two groups of professional women in government service who found some satisfaction in effective *interpersonal relationships* with their subordinates and fellow employees. In Herzberg's 'rational explanation' these innocent feelings were interpreted as 'a sickness in motivation ... brought about by the insecurity of women competing in a traditionally masculine domain'. These comments illustrate the danger that Herzberg's dichotomy between 'satisfaction' and 'dissatisfaction', job content and job context, can become a Procrustean bed upon which all experience, suitably lopped and trimmed, must be made to fit. In fact there is considerable evidence that leadership and good human relationships contribute to both work achievement and individual job satisfaction.

CRITICS OF HERZBERG'S THEORY

The hypothesis that there are exclusive sets of 'satisfiers' and 'dissatisfiers' has been denied by other empirical investigators, apart from those already mentioned. As we have seen, these writers have blurred the sharp edges of the dichotomy by showing that intrinsic factors may act as dissatisfiers and extrinsic (or contextual) factors can serve as satisfiers.[5] Industrial sociologists have confirmed this view, with suitable reservations. Alan Fox has summed up their views with the suggestion that there is a useful distinction between satisfaction *in* a job and satisfaction *with* a job.[6] Those who have attempted an impartial review of the literature in the 'Herzberg controversy' have concluded that the intrinsic-extrinsic dichotomy does not adequately reflect the sources of positive and negative attitudes to work: in short, they regard it as an over-simplification.[7]

Once the flaws in Herzberg's dichotomy between 'satisfiers' and 'dissatisfiers' became apparent, it was only a question of time before the unidimensional Maslow hierarchy would be advocated as a theoretical model for research on the shop floor.[8] In a British study of 290 female shop floor and ex-shop floor workers in electrical and electronic engineering firms it was found that 30 per cent expressed general dissatisfaction with their work. The analysis of their multi-choice questionnaires and unstructured interviews revealed the overriding importance of the work itself as a determinant of job satisfaction or dissatisfaction.[9]

R Wild and his colleagues, however, found no evidence to support Herzberg's 'principle of duality', although the practical implications were similar. In their study, the shop floor workers perceived their supervisors as being sources of both support and motivation. Wages, supportive supervision and personal relationships were contingent factors relating to lower level needs, and could be compared to Herzberg's maintenance (hygiene) factors. 'The distinctive difference between our satisfied and dissatisfied subjects lay in the lack of self-actualization perceived by the latter in relation to their work.' Those who experienced some degree of self-actualization found their work more interesting, varied, challenging, and allowing more opportunities for achievement and the use of abilities than those who felt frustrated. The fact that 30 per cent in the *same* job were dissatisfied confirms the thesis that individual attitudes and values inevitably produce different perceptions of work.

CONCLUSION

In retrospect, the research work of Herzberg and his colleagues, and the studies which his theory has provoked, confirm the view that work in industry and large organizations can be a means for at least the partial satisfaction of people's higher needs. Some support for Maslow's theory of prepotence is also afforded by the finding that if work does not provide adequate means for meeting the lower needs, it is experienced as positively dissatisfying, more so than if opportunities for more intrinsic satisfactions are missing. Herzberg's dualistic framework has a value as a stimulating and introductory visual sketchmap in teaching, but it becomes an over-simplification if taken beyond a certain point. Moreover, his apparent contradiction of Maslow turns out to be more a symptom of differences in casts of mind rather than anything more fundamental in theory.

Herzberg's particular contribution was his passionate concern for people, matched with an evangelistic fervour for the gospel that industrial work, as much as any other form of work, should serve the humanistic purpose of self-actualization. So much so that jobs which do not lend themselves to this end are to be 'enriched' until they do, or mechanized out of existence. In cases where mechanization or automation is impossible, 'hygiene factors', such as big financial rewards, must clearly be seen to be compensations for being sub-human.

With a new faith in man and some professional ingenuity, however, it will be possible to enrich most jobs so that they win more of both intrinsic satisfactions and extrinsic rewards for the worker. In keeping with the behavioural science school as a whole, Herzberg's public platform was that such job enrichment leads to more motivation, which in turn yields higher company profits.

KEY POINTS

- It is worth giving close attention to Herzberg's Motivation – Hygiene theory because there is a lot of truth in it. The factors which satisfy or motivate us at work are not the opposite of the ones that dissatisfy or demotivate us: they are not two sides of the same coin.

- The factors which make us unhappy are *around* the job itself. Using a medical metaphor, Herzberg called them the Hygiene factors. Improve these conditions and you will be reducing the level of dissatisfaction. But you won't make people happy by this route alone.

▪ To improve satisfaction (and motivation) *in* a job, as opposed to mere contentment *with* a job, you have to tackle another set of factors: *achievement, recognition, variety* and *creativity*. These Motivators, as Herzberg called them, are more intrinsic to the work itself, whereas the Hygiene factors are extrinsic. A wise manager is mindful of both sets.

▪ Financial remuneration is not merely another Hygiene factor: money straddles the divide because it is also often a tangible measure of achievement and symbol of recognition.

▪ Herzberg placed 'supervision' in the Hygiene camp – he never used the term 'leadership'. But who makes achievement possible? Who stimulates creativity? Who gives recognition? Good leaders do!

There is not one whom we employ who does not, like ourselves, desire recognition, praise, gentleness, forbearance, patience.

Henry Ward Beecher

PART 3

How to Motivate Others: The Eight Principles of Motivation

7

A Framework for Motivation

A man, woman or child is motivated when he or she *wants* to do something. Motivation covers *all* the reasons which cause a person to act, including negative ones like fear along with the more positive motives, such as money, promotion or recognition.

From the Fifty-Fifty Rule it follows that the extent to which you can motivate anyone else is limited, for 50 per cent of the cards are, so to speak, in their hands. You can provide motives or incentives in one way or another; you can offer rewards or issue threats; you can attempt to persuade. All these actual or potential influences may have an effect, for remember that 50 per cent of a person's motivation stems from the environment. If you are a leader, then you are a key factor in the environment of those who work for you. But your power is limited. As the proverb says, 'You can take a horse to water, but you cannot make him drink.'

In this chapter I have summed up what you *can* do under eight headings – the principles or rules of motivation. *How* you apply them will clearly depend upon the situation. But they stand as pillars of encouragement, both inviting you to take up your responsibility as a leader for inspiring others and pointing you in the right direction.

'I never saw a man in our profession who possessed the magic art of infusing the same spirit into others which inspired their own actions. All agree there is but one Nelson.' So wrote Admiral Lord St Vincent to Nelson in a letter, a glowing tribute from such a superior to his junior. Will the same ever be said about you?

1. BE MOTIVATED YOURSELF

The first and golden rule of motivation is that you will never inspire others unless you are inspired yourself. Only a motivated leader motivates others. Example is the great seducer.

It is so simple and so obvious, isn't it? But why is it so neglected in management today?

Enthusiasm inspires, especially when combined with trust. Its key importance can perhaps best be seen by considering its opposites. What impression would we make as leaders if we were apathetic, stolid, half-hearted, indifferent and uninterested? Enthusiasm is infectious; and enthusiasts are usually competent too, since they believe in and like what they are doing.

One of the world's first philosopher-consultants, Confucius, was once called in by a Chinese feudal king to check the corruption and theft which was rife in his domain. The fact that both the king and his court indulged in these practices, and that others were taking their cue from them, soon became apparent to Confucius, and he simply pointed out to his client the motivating influence – for good or ill – of example. 'If you did not steal yourself,' he said, 'even if you rewarded men with gold to steal they would not do it.'

Before you criticize others for lack of motivation ask yourself if your own enthusiasm for and commitment to the task in hand is sincere, visible and tangible. Have you expressed it in deeds as well as words? Are you setting a good example? For motivation is caught, not taught.

Nothing great was ever achieved without enthusiasm.

Emerson

2. SELECT PEOPLE WHO ARE HIGHLY MOTIVATED

Since it is hard to motivate people who are not already motivated it makes sense to select those who already are. It is true that in the coldest flint there is hot fire, but you may lack the skill to release such hidden sparks.

You need people working for you who, like John Bunyan, 'could not be content, unless I was found in the exercise of my gift, unto which also I was greatly animated'. Bunyan added that 'great grace and small gifts are better than great gifts and no grace', which can be translated here to mean that when you select someone for a job a high motivation and modest talent is to be preferred to considerable talent but little or no evidence of motivation.

Given the absence of any reliable psychological tests to measure motivation, managers are thrown back on their judgment. Some useful tips for interviewers are:

- Remember that someone at an interview is trying to influence or motivate you to give them the job. Some people find it easy to *act* as if they are highly motivated or enthusiastic for an hour during an interview. Others, who may be very motivated, may come across as 'laid back'.

- By their fruits you shall know them. Look for evidence in what they have done. What someone wishes to do he or she will find a way of doing. Has persistence and perseverance – evidences of high motivation – ever been shown? Ask the referees who know him or her well.

- Describe several work situations that require high motivation and ask the applicant how he or she would react.

No man will find the best way to do a thing unless he loves to do that thing.

Japanese proverb

3. TREAT EACH PERSON AS AN INDIVIDUAL

Unless you ask a person what motivates them – what they want – you will not know. We are all individuals. What motivates one person in the team may not motivate another. Enter into some sort of dialogue with each individual member of the group.

Not that individuals will always be clear about what they want. Our motivation changes with age and circumstance. One of your functions as a leader may be to help individuals to clarify what they are seeking at any given time in their careers.

A wise leader in an organization always remembers that a whole bushel of wheat is made up of single grains. By listening to individuals, giving them an opportunity to express their hopes and fears, the leader is also showing true care. The intention, however, must be to help if possible and not to manipulate. 'You would play upon me... You would seek to know my stops... You would pluck out the heart of my mystery'. That is cynical manipulation, as unmasked in Shakespeare's words.

Leadership stands in sharp contrast to such person-management. Sir John Smythe VC wrote,

A good leader is someone whom people will follow through thick and thin, In good times and bad, because they have confidence in him as a person, his ability and his knowledge of the job, and because *they know they matter to him*.

As many men, so many minds; everyone in his own way.

Terence

4. SET REALISTIC AND CHALLENGING TARGETS

'There is no inspiration in the ideals of plenty and stability,' wrote John Lancaster Spalding. People are capable of transcending self in the pursuit of high and demanding ideals.

Most people reveal this capacity in the way they respond better to a challenge. There is a fine balance here. If objectives are totally unrealistic they will demotivate people: if they are too easy to attain, on the other hand, they are also uninspiring. As a leader you have to get the balance right. 'It is not enough to do our best,' said Winston Churchill. 'Sometimes we have to do what is required.'

In 3M, for example, managers are *challenged* by demanding goals. For instance, says Lewis W Lehr, the former Chairman of 3M, in the field of innovation the targets are set to stretch all concerned:

> Our divisions shoot for a high target: In any given year, twenty five per cent of sales should come from products introduced within the last five years. Of course, not every division hits its target every year. But our managers are judged not only on their ability to make existing product lines grow but also on their knack for bringing innovative new products to market. So they have a built-in incentive to keep R&D strong.

It is essential to *agree* targets or objectives with those who have to carry them out. For the principle is true that the more we *share* decisions which affect our working lives, the more we are motivated to carry them out. If the person *accepts* that the objective is both realistic and desirable or important, then he or she will start drawing upon *their* 50 per cent of the motivational equation.

By asking the impossible we obtain the best possible.

Italian proverb

5. REMEMBER THAT PROGRESS MOTIVATES

As the ACL models suggests, we are motivated not simply by our individual needs but also by needs emanating from the common task. We *want* to finish what we are doing. The more significant the task, the stronger is the need to complete it satisfactorily. John Wesley called it 'the lust to finish'.

It is a sound principle that progress motivates. If people know that they are moving forwards it leads them to increase their efforts. We invest more in success.

Therefore it is important to ensure that people receive proper feedback. Feedback is defined in *Webster's Dictionary* as 'the return to the input of a part of the output of a machine, system or process'. Without feedback people will not know if they are moving in the right direction at the right speed.

Conversely, feedback on relative lack of progress also motivates. For it concentrates minds on what must be done if success is to be yet achieved. If you confront people with the realities of their situation in this way, then the 'law of the situation' will do the work of motivation for you.

A man grows most tired while standing still.

Chinese proverb

6. CREATE A MOTIVATING ENVIRONMENT

Although you have limited power to motivate others you can do a great deal to create an environment which they will find motivating. Most of us have experienced the flip-side of such an environment: one that *reduces* motivation. A restrictive organizational culture, which over-emphasizes controls and reduces people to passive roles, coupled with an unpredictable and irascible superior who tells off people in public, is hardly likely to bring out the best in human nature.

It is important that Herzberg's 'hygiene' factors are properly catered for. The physical and psychological well-being of people has to have a top priority. Only introduce control systems where necessary, for over-controlling does reduce motivation. Double-check that people have a proper input into the decisions that affect their working lives, especially when any substantial change is involved. Keep units or sub-units as small as possible, for large organizations tend to become bureaucratic and demotivational if they lack inspired leaders.

Lastly, pay attention to job design. Repetitive work can become boring if uninterrupted, so introduce as much variety as possible. Let people work on something they can recognize as their own product, for people find real autonomy motivates them. Ensure that the person doing the job understands its impact on others, so that they see the significance of it. That is vital, especially if you want people to be so involved that they contribute new ideas and help forward the essential process of innovation.

The creative act thrives in an environment of mutual stimulation, feedback and constructive criticism – in a community of creativity.

William T Brady

7. PROVIDE FAIR REWARDS

A lynx chasing a snow rabbit will only chase it for about 200 metres, then it gives up. For the food gained if the prey was caught will not replace the energy lost in the pursuit. Working on the same unconscious principle, it will chase a deer for longer.

All work implies this element of balancing what we give with what we expect to receive. Fairness or justice means that the return should be equivalent in value to the contribution. Performance ought to be linked to rewards, just as promotion should be related to merit.

The former – getting financial rewards fair – is easier said than done in many work situations. But the principle is still important and ways of applying it have to be found. Justinian wrote that 'Justice is the constant and unceasing will to give everyone his right or due.' That genuine and sustained intention is expected from any leader who has discretion over the distribution of rewards.

The principle has to be applied with especial care over monetary remunerations, for if fairness is not *perceived* there it can breed a lack of motivation and low morale. When remuneration is poor, workers put less effort into their jobs. Money is a key incentive. Therefore proper job evaluation schemes, involving a representative group of work people in the judgments about the financial worth of jobs, are vitally important.

There are, of course, other rewards we gain from working, as Maslow's hierarchy of needs illustrates. Opportunities for professional development and personal growth are especially valuable to good people. But money has a strategic importance for most people, not least as a measure of recognition for the significance of their contributions. As the means of exchange and as a store of wealth, money is probably the most useful material reward you can give.

He who likes cherries soon learns to climb.

German proverb

8. GIVE RECOGNITION

Despite what I have just written about money I believe that recognition is often an even more powerful motivator. As I hinted, money anyway often means more to people as a tangible symbol of recognition than as the wherewithal to buy more material goods.

This thirst for recognition is universal. In gifted people it amounts to a desire for fame or glory. For example, Isambard Brunel could write in his diary: 'My self-conceit and love of glory, or rather approbation, vie with each other which shall govern me.'

As a leader you can give recognition and show appreciation in a variety of ways. A sincere 'well done' or 'thank you' can work wonders for a person's morale.

Sir Richard Branson, chairman of the Virgin Group, said:

> My parents brought me up with lots of praise and little criti-
> cism. We all flourish with praise. Flowers do well when they
> are watered and shrivel up when they are not, and people are
> exactly the same, whether you are a chief executive or a
> switchboard operator.

But it is equally important to encourage a climate where each person recognizes the worth or value of the contribution of other members of the team. For it is recognition by our peers – discerning equals or colleagues – that we value even more than the praise of superiors. We are social animals and we thirst for the esteem of others. Without fairly regular payments by others into that deposit account it is hard to maintain the balance of our own self-esteem.

Seize every opportunity, then, to give recognition, even if it is only for effort. We cannot always command results. Perceive the worth of what the other person is doing and show your appreciation. You do not have to be a manager to do that, for true leadership can always be exercised from marginal positions.

Any of us will put out more and better ideas if our efforts are fully appreciated.

Alexander F Osborn

SUMMARY:
HOW TO MOTIVATE OTHERS

1. Be motivated yourself

2. Select people who are highly motivated

3. Treat each person as an individual

4. Set realistic and challenging targets

5. Remember that progress motivates

6. Create a motivating environment

7. Provide fair rewards

8. Give recognition

We are more easily persuaded, in general, by the reasons we ourselves discover than by those that are given to us by others.

Blaise Pascal

It is a fine thing to have ability, but the ability to discover ability in others is the true test of leadership.

Elbert Hubbard

It is no use saying 'We are doing our best.' You have got to succeed in doing what is necessary.

Winston S Churchill

KEY POINTS

Be motivated yourself

As a leader you need to be enthusiastic. You can't light a fire with a dead match! There is nothing so contagious as enthusiasm. Certainly, great designs are not accomplished without enthusiasm. As the Bedouin proverb says: *What comes from your heart is greater than what comes from your hand alone.*

Select people who are highly motivated

It is hard to motivate people who are not motivated already. Therefore look for people who have the seeds of high motivation in them already. As Oliver Cromwell once said: 'Give me the red-coated captain who knows what he is fighting for and loves what he knows.' Build your team not from those who talk enthusiastically but from those who show eagerness for the business and steady commitment in their actions.

Treat each person as an individual

Theories and principles apply to the generality of people. You will never know how they apply, even *if* they apply, to any given individuals unless you observe them and talk to them. You will learn what motivates them, and perhaps also how their pattern of motivation has changed over their lifetime. The Greek dramatist Menander once said, 'Know thyself,' which is a good saying, but not in all situations. In many it is better to say, 'Know others.' As a leader you should aspire to know others. A good shepherd knows his sheep by name.

■ *Set realistic and challenging targets*

The best people like to be stretched – they welcome feasible but demanding tasks. Don't make life too easy for them! Fortunately business life provides a series of challenges, enough to keep everyone on their toes. Without toil, trouble, difficulty and struggle there is no sense of achievement. Your skill as a leader is to set and agree goals, objectives or targets that both achieve the task and develop the team and its individual members.

■ *Remember that progress motivates*

We all need positive feedback that we are moving in the right direction, for that encourages us to persevere in the face of difficulties. 'I will go anywhere, as long as it is forwards,' said David Livingstone. If you as leader can show to your team, and to each individual member, that progress *is* being made, that in itself will feed the determination to press forwards on the path of success.

■ *Create a motivating environment*

Leadership calls for social creativity every bit as important and demanding as the artistic creativity of a painter, sculptor or composer. You are there to build teamwork, and that is a creative activity. More widely, all leaders in an organization should work together to ensure that it is an interesting, stimulating and challenging place of work. Remember the 50/50 Principle: about half of our motivation comes from outside ourselves, especially the people around us. Their commitment, passion and stimulating creative minds can awaken the sleeping powers within us. Your job as a leader is to foster that learning and motivating environment.

■ *Provide fair rewards*

We have a built-in sense of fairness. It is sometimes not easy to ensure equity in salary and bonuses, but it is important to remember that the perception of unfair rewards does have a demotivating effect on most people – Herzberg was right in that respect. As a general principle, financial (and other) rewards should match the relative value of contribution, according to the market assessment for any particular kind of work.

■ *Give recognition*

At best money is a crude measure of the value of work. Is a pop star really worth a thousand times more than a brain surgeon? A good leader should be swift to show recognition to *all* members of the team or organization, however indirect their contribution is to the overall task. You should work on the principle of 'credit where credit is due'. Where the work of people is valued there is always motivation to do it – and to do it well.

Those who are near will not hide their ability, and those who are distant will not grumble at their toil... That is what is called being a leader and teacher of men.

Hsün Tzu

Parting Reflections – Towards a New Theory of Motivation

There are two questions in this field. Why do people work? Why do they work willingly and well?

The answer of psychologists such as Maslow, McGregor and Herzberg is not an unreasonable one: we work in order to satisfy our basic and higher needs; ultimately, in the secular humanist tradition, we strive to fulfil ourselves, which in that philosophy is the end or meaning of life.

The problem with this general philosophy is that it seems to be very self-centred. We are always chain-reacting to our own set of needs. Yet Maslow had observed the paradox that it is only when people forget about their own happiness in the service of something greater than themselves, such as a worthwhile cause, they experience a measure of 'self-actualization'. If, by contrast, you do things in order to be 'self-actualized', you will miss the boat. Or, as the Bible puts it succinctly, to save your life you must be willing to lose it.

To get round this problem of escaping from the gravitational pull of self-centredness we may have to be willing to move away from a need-focused concept of motivation and think of ourselves more as being primarily motivated, sometimes inspired, by love. Here I am obviously not thinking of love as the familiar strong emotion in a family or sexual context but more as a form of positive energy present in a person that is always active in seeking good. 'Love is an orientation, a direction of energy,' Iris Murdoch once said. What could be more motivating than love?

A natural and primary object of love in that sense, of course, is one's self, for all of us seek our own good – and that of our families. To feed, clothe, house, educate and protect ourselves and our 'nearest and dearest' is always going to be a chief priority. But work can be more than a means to those important but limited ends. It can, for example, be a means of serving others and, it has been said, 'service is love in action'. Moreover, all of us want to make a contribution to add value to life. Work that enables us to do so is work that we value and we give ourselves willingly to it.

Work as a form of service requiring skill, work that calls for creativity in all its rich variety, work that fosters a deep comradeship with our co-workers, is almost by definition work that motivates us to give our best. Or, putting it differently, when, as Kahil Gibran says, 'Work is the expression of love,' then motivation will never be our problem. Perhaps the real challenge of leadership today is to locate, release and channel the power of love that flows from deep inner springs within us all.

Notes

Chapter One
1. A. H. Maslow, *Motivation and Personality* (New York, Harper and Brothers, 1954).

2. F. Herzberg, B. Mausner and B. B. Snyderman, *The Motivation to Work* (New York, John Wiley, 2nd edn, 1959) and F. Herzberg, *Work and the Nature of Man* (Cleveland, USA, World Publishing Company, 1966).

3. R. Tannenbaum and W. H. Schmidt, 'How to Choose a Leadership Pattern', *Harvard Business Review*, March–April (1958).

4. For confirmation of this point in particular, and for a discussion of sharing decisions in general, see F. A. Heller, *Managerial Decision-making: A Study of Leadership Styles and Power Sharing*, (Tavistock Publications, 1971).

Chapter Two
1.   A. H. Maslow, *Eupsychian Management: A Journal* (Richard D. Irwin, 1965).

2.   F. E. Fiedler, 'Leadership – A new model', *Discovery* (April 1965) and, *A Theory of Leadership Effectiveness* (McGraw-Hill, 1967). For an appraisal, see W. Hill, 'An Empirical Test of Fiedler's Contingency Model of Leadership Effectiveness in Three Organizations', *The Southern Journal of Business* (July 1969). See also, R. Blake and J. Mouton, *The Management Grid* (Houston, Gulf Publishing, 1964). For further examples of the situationalist approach, see Bavelas, 'Leadership: Man and Function', *Administrative Science Quarterly*, 5 (1960), 491–8, and Bales and Slater, 'Role Differentiation in Small Decision-Making Groups', in Talcott Parsons *et al.*, *Family, Socialization and Interaction Process*, (Glencoe, Free Press, 1955). For the origins of the 'styles' preoccupation (in the work of Kurt Lewin), see Lewin and Lippitt, 'An Experimental Approach to the Study of Autocracy and Democracy: A Preliminary Note', *Sociometry*, 1 (1938), 292–300.

Chapter Three
1.   N. Rudd, *T. E. Page*, Bristol Classical Press, 1983.

Chapter Four
1.   *Motivation and Personality* (1954), p. ix. All the Maslow quotations in this chapter are from this book.

2.   J. C. Smuts, *Holism and Evolution* (1926), p. ix.

Chapter Five
1.   C. N. Cofer and M. H. Appley, *Motivation: Theory and Practice* (1964).

2. *The Human Side of Enterprise*, Chapters 3 and 4.

3. R. Likert, *New Patterns of Management* (1961).

4. C. Argyris, *Personality and Organization* (1957) and *Integrating the Individual and the Organization* (1964).

5. J. H Goldthorpe *et al.*, *The Affluent Worker* (1968), p. 178.

6. M. D. Vernon, *Human Motivation* (1969), p. 161.

7. A. Fox, *A Sociology of Work in Industry* (1971), p. 10; cf. Professor J. Morris of Manchester Business School, 'The Human Meaning of Work' (unpublished paper, 1971): the important question is whether the instrumental attitude 'be established as a norm for future action or seen as a tragic sign of failed aspirations' (reported in *The Times*, 18 January 1971).

Chapter Six

1. F. Herzberg, B. Mausner, R. Peterson and D. Capwell, *Job Attitudes: Review of Research and Opinion* (1957).

2. *Motivation and Personality*, pp. 64–5, 81. Cf. Maslow's nearest approach to Herzberg's position: 'The parallel contrast in the motivational life of a single person is between growth motivation and defence motivation (homeostasis, safety motivation, the reduction of pains and losses, etc.), *Eupsychian Management* (1964), p. xii.

3. For example, Professor Liam Hudson was aware of his own tendency towards dichotomy: 'It is evident that I think in binary terms, and of tension between opposing values. This may prove a gross oversimplification... My hope of course is that there is enough in nature and the human mind that is polar to make my approach worth pursuing. If not, I can only throw up my hands – a binary

beast – and leave the field to minds more subtle,' *Frames of Mind* (1968), p. 93.

4. Others have noted the basic compatibility of the two approaches. For example, in *Work and the Nature of Man* (1968), pp. 140–1, Herzberg described a doctoral study by one of his students who had applied the motivation – hygiene theory, using a modified form of Maslow's hierarchy, to 30 rehabilitation patients in a Cleveland hospital.

5. G. Gunn, J. Veroff and S. Feld, *Americans View their Mental Health* (1959); S. H. Peres, 'An Exploration of Engineers' and Scientists' Motives as Related to Job Performance', *American Psychological Association* (1963); H. Rosen, 'Occupational Motivation of Research Workers and Development Personnel', *Personnel Administration*, Vol. 26 (1963); M. R. Malinovsky and J. R. Barry, 'Determinants of Work Attitudes', *Journal of Applied Psychology*, Vol. 49 (1965); R. B. Ewen, C. L. Hulin, P. C. Smith and E. A. Locke, 'An Empirical Test of Herzberg's Two-Factor Theory', *ibid.*, Vol. 50 (1966); C. A. Lindsay, E. Marks and L. Gorlow, 'The Herzberg Theory: A Critique and Reformulation', *ibid.*, Vol. 51 (1967); G. B. Graen, 'Testing Traditional and Two-Factor Hypotheses Concerning Job Satisfaction', *ibid.*, Vol. 52 (1968); W. W. Ronan, 'Relative Importance of Job Characteristics', and 'Individual and Situational Variables Relating to Job Satisfaction, *ibid.*, Vol. 54 (1970).

6. *A Sociology of Work in Industry* (1971), p. 23.

7. R. J. Burke, 'Are Herzberg's Motivators and Hygienes Unidimensional?', *Journal of Applied Psychology*, Vol. 50 (1966); D. A. Wood and W. K. LeBold, 'The Multivariate Nature of Professional Job Satisfaction', *Personnel Psychology*, Vol. 23 (1970).

8. R. Payne, 'Factor Analysis of a Maslow-Type Need Satisfaction Questionnaire', *Personnel Psychology*, Vol. 25 (1970).

9. R. Wild, A. B. Hill and C. C. Ridgeway, 'Job Satisfaction and Labour Turnover amongst Women Workers', *The Journal of Management Studies*, Vol. 7 (1970).

Further Reading

Adler, A, *The Science of Living*, George Allen & Unwin, 1930

Adler, A, *Social Interest: A Challenge to Mankind* (Translated by J Linton and R Vaughan), Faber & Faber, 1937

Alderfer, A, *Existence, Relatedness and Growth: Human Needs in Organizations*, New York, Free Press, 1972

Arendt, H, *The Human Condition*, University of Chicago, 1958

Argyris, C, *Personality and Organization: The Conflict between System and the Individual*, Harper & Row, 1957

Argyris, C, *Integrating the Individual and the Organization*, Wiley, 1964

Barnes, M C, Fogg, A H, Stephens, C N and Titman, L G, *Company Organization: Theory and Practice*, George Allen & Unwin, 1970

Berger, P L (ed), *The Human Shape of Work: Studies in the Sociology of Occupations*, Macmillan, 1964

Blauner, R, *Alienation and Freedom: The Factory Worker and his Industry*, University of Chicago, 1964

Blaum, M L and Naylor, J C, *Industrial Psychology*, New York, Harper & Row, 1968

Borne, E and Henry, F, *A Philosophy of Work* (Translated by F Jackson), Sheed & Ward, 1938

Bottome, P, *Alfred Adler: Apostle of Freedom*, Faber and Faber, 3rd edn, 1957

Brown, J A C, *The Social Psychology of Industry: Human Relations in the Factory*, Penguin, 1954

Burns, T (ed), *Industrial Man*, Penguin, 1969

Campbell, J P, and others, *Managerial Behaviour, Performance and Effectiveness*, McGraw-Hill, 1970

Child, J, *British Management Thought: A Critical Analysis*, George Allen & Unwin, 1969

Cofer, C N and Appley, M H, *Motivation: Theory and Practice*, Wiley, 1964

Edholm, O G, *The Biology of Work*, Weidenfeld & Nicolson, 1967

Emmett, D, *Function, Purpose and Powers: Some Concepts in the Study of Individuals and Societies*, Macmillan, 1958

Ford, R N, *Motivation through Work Itself*, American Management Association, 1969

Fox, A, *A Sociology of Work in Industry*, Collier-Macmillan, 1971.

Fraser, R (ed) *Work: Twenty Personal Accounts*, Penguin, 1954

Friedmann, G, *The Anatomy of Work: The Implications of Specialization*, Heinemann, 1961

Fromm, E, *Marx's Concept of Man*, Frederick Ungar, 1961

Furst, L R, *Romanticism in Perspective*, Macmillan, 1970

Gardner, J W, *Self-Renewal: The Individual and the Innovative Society*, Harper & Row, 1963

Gellerman, S W, *Motivation and Productivity*, American Management Association, 1963

Gellerman, S W, *Management by Motivation*, American Management Association, 1968

Goldstein, K, *The Organism*, American Book, 1939

Goldstein, K, *Human Nature in the Light of Psychopathology*, Harvard University Press, 1940

Goldthorpe, J, Lockwood, D, Bechhofer, F and Platt, J, *The Affluent Worker: Industrial Attitudes and Behaviour*, Cambridge University Press, 1968

Gough, J W, *The Rise of the Entrepreneur*, Batsford, 1969

Goyder, G, *The Responsible Company*, Blackwell, 1961

Gunn, G, Veroff, J and Feld, S, *Americans View Their Mental Health*, Basic Books, 1959

Hahn, C P, *Dimensions of Job Satisfaction and Career Motivation*, Pittsburg, American Institute of Research, 1959

Herzberg, F, Mausner, B, Peterson, R and Capwel, D, *Job Attitudes: Review of Research and Opinion*, Psychological Service of Pittsburg, 1957

Ivens, M (ed), *Industry and Values: The Objectives and Responsibilities of Business*, Harrap, 1970

Jung, C, *Modern Man in Search of a Soul*, Harcourt, Brace & Co., 1933

Jung, C, *The Integration of the Personality*, Routledge & Kegan Paul, 1950

Katz, D and Kahn, R L, *The Social Psychology of Organizations*, Wiley, (2nd edn, 1978)

Klein, L, *The Meaning of Work*, The Fabian Society, 1963

Lamont, C, *The Philosophy of Humanism*, Barrie & Rockliff, 5th edn, 1965

Lawler, E E, *Motivation in Work Organizations*, Brooks–Cole, 1973

Likert, R, *New Patterns of Management*, McGraw-Hill, 1961

Lubac, H de, *The Drama of Atheist Humanism*, Sheed & Ward, 1947

Lupton, T, *On the Shop Floor*, Pergamon, 1963

Lupton, T, *Management and the Social Sciences*, Hutchinson, 1966

Macmurray, J, *The Self as Agent* and *Persons in Relation*, Faber & Faber, 1957 and 1961. Gifford Lectures, 1953–4

Maslow, A H (ed), *New Knowledge in Human Values*, Harper & Bros, 1959

Maslow, A H, *Religions, Values, and Peak-Experiences*, Ohio State University Press, 1964

Maslow, A H, *Eupsychian Management: A Journal*, Richard D. Irwin and the Dorsey Press, 1965

Maslow, A H, *Toward a Psychology of Being*, Van Nostrand Reinhold, 2nd edn, 1968

Mayo, E, *The Human Problems of an Industrial Civilization*, Macmillan, 1933

Mayo, E, *The Social Problems of an Industrial Civilization*, Harvard University Press, 1945

McClelland, D C et al., *The Achievement Motive*, Appleton-Century-Crofts, 1953

McClelland, D C, *The Achieving Society*, Van Nostrand, 1961

O'Brien, R H, Dickinson, A M and Rosow, M P, *Industrial Behaviour Modification: A Learning-based Approach to Industrial Organizational Problems*, Pergamon, 1982

O'Toole, J, *Work in America*, MIT Press, 1973

Passmore, J, *The Perfectibility of Man*, Duckworth, 1970

Paul, W J and Robertson, K B, *Job Enrichment and Employee Motivation*, Gower Press, 1970

Robertson, I T and Smith, M, *Motivation and Job Design: Theory, Research and Practice*, Institute of Personnel Management, 1985

Roethlisberger, F J and Dickson, W J, *Management and the Worker*, Harvard University Press, 1959

Rogers, C, *Counselling and Psychotherapy*, Houghton Mifflin, 1942

Rogers, C, *Client Centred Therapy*, Houghton Mifflin, 1951

Rogers, C, *On Becoming a Person: A Therapist's View of Psychotherapy*, London, Constable, 1961

Sayles, L R, *Behaviour of Industrial Work Groups*, John Wiley, 1958

Schacht, R, *Alienation*, Allen & Unwin, 1971

Schein, E H, *Organizational Psychology*, Englewood Cliffs, NJ, Prentice-Hall, 1980

Smigel, E O (ed), *Work and Leisure: A Contemporary Social Problem*, New Haven (Connecticut), College and University Press, 1963

Steers, R M and Porter, L W, *Motivation and Work Behavior*, New York, McGraw-Hill, 1979

Tannenbaum, A S, *Social Psychology of the Work Organization*, California, Wadsworth; and London, Tavistock, 1966

Tilgher, A, *Work: What it has meant to men through the ages* (translated from Italian by D C Fisher), Harraps, 1931

Turner, A N and Lawrence, P, *Industrial Jobs and the Worker*, Harvard University Press, 1965

Vernon, M D, *Human Motivation*, Cambridge University Press, 1969

Vroom, V H, *Work and Motivation*, John Wiley, 1964

Weick, K E, *The Social Psychology of Organizing*, Addison–Wesley, 1979

Whyte, W F, *Money and Motivation*, Harper & Bros, 1955

Whyte, W F, *Men at Work*, Irwin & Dorsey, 1961

On leadership

Adair, J, *The Inspirational Leader*, Kogan Page, 2005

Adair, J, *Not Bosses But Leaders*, Kogan Page, 3rd edn, 2006

Adair, J, *How to Grow Leaders*, Kogan Page, 2006

The classic books on motivation

Herzberg, F, *Work and the Nature of Man*, London, Stapels Press, 1968 (Published in America in 1966)

Herzberg, F, Mausner, B and Snyderman, B B, *The Motivation to Work*, John Wiley & Sons, 2nd edn, 1959

Maslow, A H, *Motivation and Personality*, Harper & Row, 1954

McGregor, D, *The Human Side of Enterprise*, McGraw Hill, 1960

Index

italic indicates a figure in the text

ALSO AVAILABLE FROM KOGAN PAGE

"One of the foremost thinkers on leadership in the world." Sir John Harvey-Jones

0 7494 4919 5   Paperback   2007

ALSO AVAILABLE FROM KOGAN PAGE

"Every practising leader can benefit from this readable book."
Warren Bennis, Distinguished Professor of Management, University of Southern California

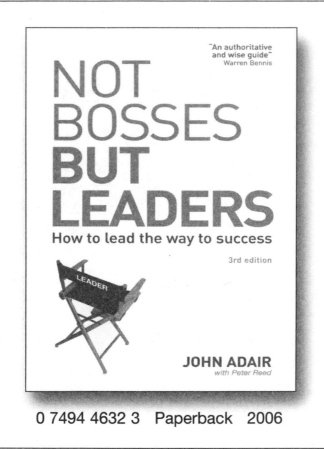

"An authoritative and wise guide"
Warren Bennis

NOT BOSSES BUT LEADERS

How to lead the way to success

3rd edition

LEADER

JOHN ADAIR
with Peter Reed

0 7494 4632 3   Paperback   2006

ALSO AVAILABLE FROM KOGAN PAGE

"A positive, thought-provoking work that should encourage and inspire the reader to self-assess – an important step on the road to becoming a better leader." Management Today

0 7494 4456 8   Paperback   2005

ALSO AVAILABLE FROM KOGAN PAGE

"Sets out practical and realistic theories and strategies underpinned by examples from his lifetime of involvement with leadership education."
Edge

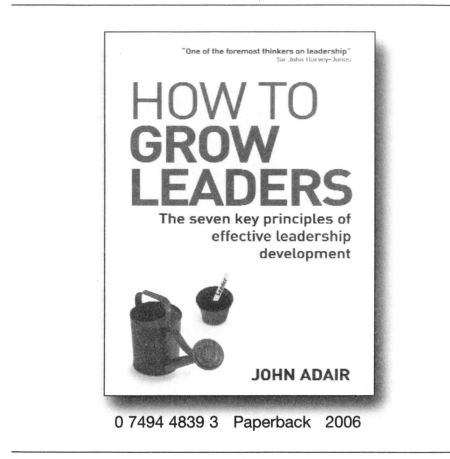

0 7494 4839 3   Paperback   2006

FURTHER READING FROM KOGAN PAGE

Leadership Crash Course: How to Create Personal Leadership Value, 2nd edition, by Paul Taffinder

Making Sense of Management, by Ester Cameron and Mike Green

Management Stripped Bare: What They Don't Teach You at Business School, 2nd edition, by Jo Owen

Motivate to Win: How to Motivate Yourself and Others, 3rd edition, by Richard Denny

My Big Idea, by Rachel Bridge

Running Board Meetings: Tips and Techniques for Getting the Best From Them, 3rd edition, by Patrick Dunne

The Successful Entrepreneur's Guidebook: Where you are Now, Where you want to be & How to get there, by C Barrow, R Brown and L Clarke

Ultimate Business Presentations Book, by Martin Yale and Peter Sander

KOGAN PAGE *CREATING SUCCESS* SERIES

Be Positive, 2nd edition, by Phil Clements

Better Business Writing by Timothy R V Foster

Dealing With Difficult People by Roy Lilley

Develop Your Assertiveness, 2nd edition, by Sue Bishop

Develop Your NLP Skills, 2nd edition, by Andrew Bradbury

The Effective Leader by Rupert Eales-White

How to Manage Meetings by Alan Barker

How to Motivate People, 2nd edition, by Patrick Forsyth

How to Negotiate Effectively by David Oliver

How to Understand Business Finance by Bob Cinnamon and Brian Helweg-Larsen

How to Write a Business Plan, 2nd edition, by Brian Finch

How to Write a Marketing Plan, 2nd edition, by John Westwood

How to Write Reports and Proposals, 2nd edition, by Patrick Forsyth

Improve Your Communication Skills by Alan Barker
Organise Yourself, 2nd edition, by John Caunt
Successful Presentation Skills, 3rd edition, by Andrew Bradbury
Successful Project Management, 2nd edition, by Trevor Young
Successful Time Management by Patrick Forsyth
Taking Minutes of Meetings, 2nd edition, by Joanna Gutmann
Understanding Brands by Peter Cheverton

The above titles are available from all good bookshops. For further information on these and other Kogan Page titles, or to order online, visit the Kogan Page website as **www.kogan-page.co.uk**

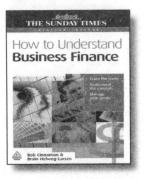